# Quantum Yoga and Mystery of Meditation

Brajendra Nath Roy

© **Brajendra Nath Roy 2022**

**All rights reserved**

All rights reserved by author. No part of this publication may be reproduced, stored in a retrieval system or transmitted in any form or by any means, electronic, mechanical, photocopying, recording or otherwise, without the prior permission of the author.

Although every precaution has been taken to verify the accuracy of the information contained herein, the author and publisher assume no responsibility for any errors or omissions. No liability is assumed for damages that may result from the use of information contained within.

First Published in March 2022

**ISBN: 978-93-93809-49-0**

**BLUEROSE PUBLISHERS**
www.bluerosepublishers.com
info@bluerosepublishers.com
+91 8882 898 898

**Cover Design:**
Muskan

**Typographic Design:**
Namrata Saini

**Distributed by:** BlueRose, Amazon, Flipkart,

"NA TASYA ROGO, NA ZARA NA MRITYU PRAPTASYA YOGAGNIMAYAM SHARIRAM."

-Sweteshwar upnishad

**BODY BAKED IN THE FIRE OF YOGA SHALL BE FREE FROM AFFLICTIONS OF DESEASE, OLD AGE AND DEATH.**

**THE BOOK IS DEDICATED TO MY GRANDCHILDREN,**

**ARJUN, NARAYAN, ARYAN & NEIL**

# CONTENTS

*Acknowledgement* ........................................................... *vii*
*Introduction*................................................................... *xii*

Why is Yoga Different? ................................... 1
Patanjali's Ashtha (Eight Limbs) of Yoga .......... 14
Pratyahar. ..................................................... 87
Dharana (Concentration) .............................. 90
Dhyan (Meditation) ....................................... 94
Samadhi ....................................................... 103
Appendix 1 ................................................... 139
Appendix 2 ................................................... 141
Appendix 3 ................................................... 144
Quantum Yoga .............................................. 147
Reference ..................................................... 162
Some Selected Yoga Postures ....................... 164

# ACKNOWLEDGEMENT

My most humble gratitude is to God for his infinite mercy that I could start and finish this task.

My next gratitude is to Sage Patanjali for such a comprehensive step by step elucidation of the philosophy, science and art of Astha yoga that will be valid and beneficial at all time and place.

I am highly indebted to Yoga Guru B.K.S.Iyengar who through his numerous writings, teaching and explicit exhibits has guided me through these years of learning and practicing yoga.

Unreserved appreciation and credit goes to Yoga Guru, Baba Ramdeo for his untiring effort in making Yoga universally acceptable as a tool to good health and prosperity.

Universal acceptability of Yoga was obtained with the declaration of 21 June as international Yoga day by United Nations. Thanks to the Prime Minister, Honourable Sri. Narendra Modi for putting it on his agenda while addressing the UNGA.

My gratitude is also to the authors of the books enlisted at the end for the material wisdom that helped me in better understanding of the subject.

All the above plus the solitude of Covid provided the impetus to write this ' work to do' book.

My unbound gratitude to the environment of my village Malsa, in Ghazipur district of Uttar Pradesh where I spent my formative four years of childhood(10 to 14) learning through tales about our scriptures and observing the conduct, values and routine practiced by the elders. Those indelible memories are still my asset and far more valuable compared to all the higher institutional learning, positions held and skills developed.

Early in 2020 my close friend from our college days, Suresh, now Dr. Suresh Chander in Washington, U.S.A. sent a message. He desired if I could write some pieces of articles related to yoga. It was meant for the magazine, 'Marg' that he initiated sixteen years back. His aim was and is to keep the young American Indians in know of the essence and value of yoga. His modest, unassuming request was captivating. I could not say 'no'. I did write and transmitted few pages.

While in the thick of everything else the world faced a new situation. Covid19 or Corona engulfed the entire globe. And a compulsory stay at home orders were passed under the name 'Lockdown'. I thought why not utilise this imposed 'be at home' situation to write a book. The result is in the reader's hand. I can guarantee the book carries no virus.

As always in this kind of work one needs the support of friends and family. During the course of thinking and writing the initial draft I often indulged into discussion with wide range of people closely known and associated with. Interestingly I found, at all level and all the time, an enthusiastic response. It was quite reassuring and helped me to accomplish this work. To mention all will be a long list. But it will be unjust not to mention those who were more often on my communication radar. They are;

Engr. Yogendra Gupta, the whatsapp group of ex –Lagosians and Rocking Rai's ( amongst the lot Maj. Gen S.P. Rai contributed his fair time and thought).

I must express my unreserved reverence and gratitude to my elder brother Sri. S.N.Roy for his encouragement, support and blessings.

I have no words to qualify my gratitude to my late wife Anand Prabha who urged (her memory continues to inspire) me to read, think, practice, write and share my experiences for whatever benefit it can render to the society.

# INTRODUCTION

Yoga today needs no introduction. Every nation and society overtly or covertly recognises the importance of yoga as an individual and collective necessity. The majority feel it is good for health. Those keen to learn more try to find its scientific base. Their efforts go beyond physical and health benefits. There are others trying for peace and tranquillity through mind control using the discipline of yoga. There are still others who go deep into the philosophy of yoga and the mystical power it generates. Lastly, there are those who take it as a journey into the spiritual world. It is believed to be a tool to liberation, *Moksha*. The last one is primarily a concept in Hinduism. Possibly this alone may be the reason why the word yoga gives it the Hindu identity.

Yoga addresses the two most vital needs of any individual: physical well-being and spiritual advancement. The idea of physical well-being does not involve arguments and discussions to establish its veracity. The spiritual aspect is always subject to arguments, philosophical and scientific logic. Rational logic can be a good start to spiritual understanding, but logic by itself alone can never experience or determine the final outcome of spiritualism. Unlike the world of science, where external observation, assumption, and experiments form the basis of knowledge, in the spiritual world, the individual body and its various constituents provide the means and methods of truth realisation. In this book, an attempt has been made to address both aspects of human life, physical and spiritual, in as simple and lucid manner as possible. Emphasis is more on the technique and viability of the various practices instead of the intricacies of philosophy. The book aims at read, learn, do and feel principles.

It is believed that yoga was first elaborately dealt with by Sage Patanjali (200 to 500 BCE) in his book *Yoga Darshan*. Going a little back, the essence of yoga in various formats, that is, *Karma Yoga*, *Gyan Yoga*, *Bhakti Yoga*, and *Shankhya Yoga* was explained at the battlefield of Kurukshetra by Lord Krishna. That was in the year 3138 BCE. It was in the form of question and answers between warrior Arjun and Lord Krishna. The complete version of the epic teaching is now the Holy Book of *Bhagavad Gita*. The most intriguing aspect of this episode is that the philosophy of peace and salvation of soul was being expounded through justification of fighting one of the fiercest wars in the history of mankind.

There is also a reference to Yoga Vasistha. Here, the sage Vasistha imparts the knowledge of yoga to Ram, an incarnation of Lord Vishnu. That was in *Treta Yuga*. It lasted from 2,165,127 BCE to 869,122 BCE. One *yuga* is a unit of reckoning time. It is equal to 432,000 earthly years. According to the Hindu scriptures life on earth that includes all animate and inanimate creation is limitless but not endless. It is cyclical in nature. One cycle is made up of four *yugas*: *Satya Yuga, Treta Yuga, Dwaper Yuga* and *Kali Yuga*. Together, these sum up to 4,320,000 years. One thousand cycles is a period of active existence followed by a similar cycle of inactive or a dormant or inactive state. By regression mechanism it will be found that yoga is as old as life and time. Life and time are eternal. So is yoga.

A similar assertion can be found in the Greek philosophy under the 'Doctrine of Universal Cycle' by Plato (429 BCE). His statement that if one can travel from eternity to eternity all probabilities would become a certainty, bears great significance to the cyclical nature of the universe. It conforms to the teachings of the great Indian sages far back in time.

Besides being eternal, yoga is also universal (*sarvabhaumya*). Everything and every act is either yoga or a product of yoga. The creation of the universe is through *Yoga Shakti* of the Brahma. Science terms it as consciousness. Believers simply call it Energy or Sound as the primal source of the universe. The common thread passing through everything is energy. Cosmos with all its constituents is pure manifestation of energy. And energy, individual or cosmic, is essentially the prime focus in yoga. In quantum mechanics, the branch of Physics dealing with the pattern of behaviour of subatomic particles, the entire Universe is Energy or its manifestation. This is the reason why the title of this book starts with the word Quantum. In the chapter titled, "Quantum Yoga" put at the end an effort has been made to derive the conjunction of the words, "Quantum Yoga."

The purpose of this book is to understand the philosophy, science and art of yoga. Yoga, in context to the present time is being practiced as an exercise. Often it is also taught as an exercise for the masses. It is designed to fit into the modern business concept. In reality Yoga is neither an exercise nor it is a mass event. Any discipline of yoga is relaxation with grace and tranquillity. Every movement involved has to be firm, steady, and slow. Every act must relate to the conscious awareness. Act without awareness is just an act; the same act with awareness becomes yoga. Certain disciplines of yoga involve no physical movement except the breath. This kind of yoga is possible only in an environment of peace unaffected by external sources.

The second and possibly the most critical aspect of yoga I wish to touch upon is meditation. Meditation is not only a buzz word. Today it is probably the most valuable, unregistered trademark for yoga. Anyone and everyone, young or old, political leaders, business tycoons, CEOs, executives, entrepreneurs, men, and women see some kind of panacea in meditation. Truely speaking meditation is the penultimate stage of *Astha Yoga*. It has its bliss and risk too. This has been extensively dealt with in the section under "Meditation and Sadhana."

Meditation is an arduous task. It is a state in which the mind, intellect and senses get devoid of any purpose and the soul is awakened. The gross body with its three Gunas (satogun, rajogun, tamogun) become non-existent and the practitioner is at the point of divine enlightenment. This is the ultimate aim of every practitioner of yoga. At the same time it is the rarest of the rare that achieve this state. An indicative probability of reaching this stage is given in the write up that follows. The rarity is on account of high level of discipline and all round fitness physical, physiological and mental it demands. Those who have not appropriately practiced and acquired the benefits from the principles preceding meditation that is, Yama, Niyam, Asana, Pranayam, Pratyahar and Dharana (concentration) can experience discomfort of disproportionate magnitude due to high energy generation and movement. It may cause long term damage. It may be worth to mention in passing that as one progresses through the phases of yoga the energy centres awaken. Awakening of these centres causes release of energy. Occasional feel of partial or total void is like stumbling on a diamond ore while walking. It should not be equated to the one resulting from meditation. One can experience flash of such moments through music, dance, chanting or even prolonged silence. Music, dance, and chanting do have their space in spiritual life. One may experience momentary sense of peace, pleasure and absence of Gunas. But it will be unsustainable and illusory. In reality it can be a state of mind void of reason and thinking and short lived. To achieve benefit of spiritual consciousness rigorous and prolonged meditation is the only way. In meditation, noise or silence is within. Meditation itself has stages. It begins with a deep concentration on an object or an image outside the body. Gradually, the object shifts to the body. Finally, it is a concentration on nothing. Add to it the duration a practitioner can firmly establish him/herself in this state of sustained intensity of concentration. The duration starts from two hours at a stretch to 10 hours. With continued practice, it becomes a part of nature. There can be exceptions with an accelerated outcome. But these are rare and invariably relate to carry forward of the past *karmas*.

During the course of writing this book, my curiosity grew to learn more about the liberation of the soul, renunciation, the concepts of *Karm Mukta* (deeds without desire), and *Jeevan Mukta* (one with no desire, not even that of liberation). Stated below is an indicative probability of reaching the door of divinity leading to the sense of realisation of a light of unmatched colour and quality.

Out of a population of 10,000,000, one will be a religious person (*karma mukta*).

Out of 10,000,000, religious persons, there will be one with a total sense of Vairag (renunciation).

From 10,000,000 persons, with *Vairag* there will be one with real wisdom (includes knowledge of self and Supreme).

From 10,000,000 persons with wisdom, one will attain liberation (state of intense meditation leading to *Samadhi*).

From 10,000,000 liberated souls, one will attain the place in the kingdom of The Supreme Godhead (*Jeevan Mukta*).

These are formidable figures even for an arithmetical genius. My aim is not to convey meditation as an unattainable feature. The purpose is to convey the right nature of meditation and the preparedness it requires. An effort has been made in this book to provide a step-by-step guide to meditation. Appendix 2 of the book will be useful for those with an advanced stage of spiritual meditation.

A few words for those who I believe have diluted the path and purpose of yoga. In the epic *Ramcharitmanas*, there is an extensive description of how religion and renunciation will be practiced in *Kaliyug*, the time frame we are in. Here are a few verses readers may find relevant.

> *Bahu dam savarahin dham jati,*
> *Vishya hari linhi na rahi virati.*

*Tapasi dhanvant daridra grihi,*

*Kali kautik tat na jat kahi*

Like the *Bhagavad Gita*, *Ramcharitmanas* is another holy book extensively liked and read in the North Indian States. It was written in the sixteenth century in Awadhi language (resembles Hindi).

The meaning of the above verse is:

In *Kaliyuga*, the *sanyasi* (one presumed to have attained renunciation) who is supposed to lead a life of austerity, will live in luxury, and acquire wealth. The traditional land owners and the farmers will be poor and will live in austerity. These are strange times!

Another one from the same epic book:

*Nirachar jo shruti path tyagi,*

*Kaliyug soi gyani so viragi.*

*Jake nakh aur jata vishala,*

*Soi tapas prashidha kalikala*

Persons who have wavered from the path of religious conduct and adopted an unethical, immoral life will be considered wise and austere. Those with long nails and long hair locks will be treated a great *Tapasvi* (an ascetic in pursuit of spiritual wisdom).

Through this book an effort has been made to convey the simple philosophy, science and art of yoga in a precise and actionable manner. It is for the reader to interpret and adopt the appropriate principles and practice. It is not important what the author perceives and writes. What matters is what the reader considers adoptable and gives it a trial in his/her routine. What follows will amply prove the freedom of reader to interpret and accept even the Holy books and epic like treatise. Srimad Bhagwat *Gita* carries only 700 verses. Most of these are in two half-lines. A book with 35 pages can contain the whole text. *Patanjali Yoga Sutras* are only 196 in number. Most of these are one-liners. The whole lot can be printed in ten pages. Both these epic works however have been expanded in thousands of pages over time. Writers have limitations. Readers have absolute freedom to accept, reject or expand.

At the end of the book, there is an article on Quantum Yoga. Quantum Yoga is precisely an Energy concept of yoga and God. *Patanjali Yoga* System also lays great emphasis on the concept of energy in its various formats, be it through food and drinks we take, the breath we inhale or thought energy we generate through meditation and *Sadhana* of *Samadhi*. In the article, I have tried to establish the convergence of the philosophy of science with the eastern thoughts of yoga (with special reference to *Patanjali Astha Yoga*). In the world of science, quantum theory states the dual behaviour of fundamental particles as energy and mass. It has further confirmed that in the end the entire Universe is either energy or its manifestation. Something precisely what the philosophy of yoga says about the *Prakriti*, the Cosmos with all its constituents. There is also a mention of Cosmic Energy and Cosmic Consciousness as the nature of God, omnipotent and omnipresent. It is owing to this similarity that the title of the book bears the word**, 'Quantum'.**

An Important Appeal

We are all endowed with varying degree of potential in our physical and mental abilities and performance. We can improve upon these through the right routine and training. Yet, our achievements will remain different. Similarly, our potential in the spiritual world will be different. Even with the best *guru*, guidance and practice one may not reach the desired destination. The slogan, 'it is not important to win, what is important is to participate,' is popular in the sporting world. The same adage is true in spiritual pursuit. It is not necessary that all will attain salvation. However, at whatever stage one is, he/she will be with more energy, vigour, and strength. These are as much needed to be successful in the material world as in the spiritual world. Therefore, my sincere urge will be to begin from stage one and see how far it propels you.

**Another important appeal is the choice of environment to practice yoga. One needs a *guru* to learn, but one does not need a *guru* to practice. If you practice all the time under instruction you are with the**

**instructor instead of being with the yoga. Better practice in isolation. Be your own *guru*. Do consult when in difficulty or doubt. For the same reason, mass yoga is not advisable. Any external source that can distract the attention is a detriment.**

Dear reader, the elucidation ends there. I have tried to share the essence of my understanding of quantum yoga and the mystery of meditation in as simple a language as possible. It must however be made abundantly clear that the final word will always be yours, the practitioner. As we progress in our pursuit from simple principles to action, from information gathering to knowledge and wisdom individual experience and expression will be the answer. Such experiences and expressions **are** dynamic in nature. These may be different at different stages. These will be valid until you feel different. In the end if you are persistent and His Grace is upon you the ultimate Truth will be realised. That will be the end point. It does not alter till eternity.

It is therefore, your experience that will carry it forward to the next generation with a new dynamism.

In the tangible world, the practice of yoga will render an affliction-free robust body and a peaceful mind. In the spiritual world, one will achieve eternal peace and freedom.

# WHY IS YOGA DIFFERENT?

Humans are the most wonderful creation whether by strategic design or through evolution.

Of all the creatures homo_ sapiens possess the most remarkable learning processes. This has enabled human species to survive and evolve even under difficult and sometimes extremely unfavourable conditions. This ability to survive begins with the birth of a child. The moment a child encounters the outside world, he/she cries. There are several speculations about the first cry of the child. One presumption is that the child senses the agony and afflictions a human body will suffer. Therefore, it is a cry of impending grief. Some believe it is a pronouncement of life. Yet, there are those who think it is the child's first and instinctive communication with the Cosmos. The child inhales the first breath and with it the vital life- force (*pran*). What is the source of this vital life- force called *pran*? In a yoga concept it is cosmic energy having a universal spread. In Hindu spiritual concept it is the soul, part of the Supreme Soul. We shall find a detailed explanation in subsequent chapters.

All religious faiths of the world believe in the theory of a creator and the creation. The form and nature of the creator and the philosophy of religions though differ. The Abrahamic concept of God is through the prophet Abraham and his sons/grandsons. The three major off-shoots of the Abrahamic religion are: Judaism founded in 7th century BCE, Christianity in the 1st century CE and Islam in the 7th century CE. The followers of these three religions believe that Abraham and his progeny play a key role in the spiritual development of individuals. Their ethical teachings are almost identical. The authority to preach and administer the ethical values and rituals is though hierarchical.

Hinduism is one of the oldest religions in the world. A popular belief is in it being *Sanatan* - timeless, eternal. Over time, it has undergone a transformation of a significant nature. From a pure knowledge concept of a formless form to the concept of incarnation (avatar), creation of numerous faith-based deities empowered with special task and abilities. Different kinds of rituals and practices have evolved to identify with or pay obeisance to respective deities. Various schools of thoughts have sprung up from time to time. And the process is one endless chain. This is the utmost freedom Hinduism grants to its believers and non-believers too. By doing so, it has acquired the power of resilience against all odds. It is a testimony to the great vision that ancient Hindu sages had. The concept is based on the premise that everyone has the potential to attain spiritual freedom and acquire divine qualities. It is so well characterised in the following Vedic *mantras*:

'*Aham tatwam Asi*' I (signifies the Brahman, supreme God) am within you (the *purush*, individual). It is believed that when a disciple enters the school to acquire knowledge and skill, he implores his *guru*, 'Can I know God (Brahman)?' The teacher replies, '*Aham tatwam Asi*' I am within you.

At the end of the academic session, the student is set to depart. He goes to the teacher to seek his permission and blessings. The teacher asks the student, 'Could you understand Brahman (God)?' The student replies, '*Aham Brahmasmi.*' (I am Brahman, the supreme knowledge.)

The two short conversations sound the magnificent ethos of Hinduism. Let us add one more from Rg. Ved. It is also referred in the *Maha Upnishad*:

*Ekam sat vipra bahudha vadanti*

The meaning is, 'Truth (God) is only one the people of wisdom call it by various names.'

It reminds me of the famous story of a chameleon.

A gentleman went for a walk to the forest. He was enamoured with the beauty and serenity of the place. He decided to spend some time there and sat under a tree on the bank of the river. Up on the tree he saw a green-coloured chameleon. He had never seen a chameleon before. On returning to his village he narrated the incident amongst his family and friends. It generated interest in others. Another person decided to go and see the creature. He did see the chameleon but with a red colour. On his return he narrated his part of the incident adding though, that the colour he saw was red. It generated further interest. Others too decided to go. Each one saw a different colour. There was a man watching the event. He went up to the little gathering and enquired the reason they had flocked together. He told them that he resided in the forest and knew about the inhabitants. He then told them that the creature was called chameleon and that it kept changing its colour.

There are numerous such tales that we all have read or heard from our elders. The universal message is, *Ekam sat vipra bahudha vadanti:* Truth is singular. The way to realising it may be different.

Knowledge of the Brahman, the absolute or the universal consciousness falls in the category of metaphysics in the world of science. In the world of religion it is known as a spiritual pursuit. In both these instances the realisation of the ultimate is personal and subjective. Though there is no universally accepted way to get to the end, we shall try to enumerate some of the established practices in Hinduism. We shall commence the journey with the learning process from childhood onwards.

## The Learning Process of a Child

At this stage of learning we shall keep aside the theory and concept of Cosmos and the knowledge of the Absolute. We shall confine ourselves to our limited surroundings that normal vision can survey and the mind can comprehend. In the scientific term we refer it as 'Zone of Middle Dimension.'

A child's learning begins and progresses in the following sequence:

-Introductory stage (*parichaya*)

At this stage, the child, with the help of elders, learns to know the name of all that senses (see, hear, smell, touch, and taste) can identify. He/she learns to differentiate based on the colour and shape of matter and mass cast in the child's memory. These imprints last until consciousness lasts. This is followed by knowledge (*Gyan*) stage.

-Knowledge (*gyan*) stage:

At this stage, the child learns the different qualities and possible uses and application of the individual items and their components. This knowledge supports the emergent evolution of humankind. Next to it is the *vigyan* (scientific approach).

-Scientific (*vigyan*) approach to knowledge:

The child has come of age. There is a heightened quest to know more. Questions like the building blocks of all matter, life cycle, relative relevance of mass and energy in the overall ecosystem etc. create ripples in the child's mind. Science is born. An endless chain of experiments and mathematical equations evolve. Postulates and theories develop. Collective validation establishes the laws and principles of Science. A new era emerges to challenge the theory and philosophy of metaphysics and spiritualism. Science and its offshoot – technology occupy an increasing space in human existence. Our survival and growth, our basic needs for wild fantasy, all appear to be easy and achievable. We want to win over death, be eternal. At the same time we are busy creating weapons of mass destruction of unimaginable power. (Just think of the U.S. nuclear device B-41capacity 25-mega tons or Russian RDS-220 hydrogen bomb capacity 50-mega tons. Compare these with the one dropped at Hiroshima with a meagre capacity of 15,000 tons.). It speaks of contradiction. The aim is to create, preserve and destroy the universe through Science. But the nearer we think we are the further it recedes. Some of the big brains in the world of Science, like Albert Einstein, Stephen Hawking, Rene Descartes, to name a few, realised the fallacy and limitations of Science. They wished to know the mind of God and the idea of God as a perfect Being. More on this subject has been dealt with in the paper, *Quantum Yoga*, at the end of this book. Science by its nature will tread the path of proof. Self experience or spiritual revelation can never be part of scientific validation. Yet, world of science does not deny the spiritual or mystical path though occasionally with certain degree of reluctance. Often our ignorance refuses to accept our limitations. One major cause of lack of awareness to spiritual awakening is that it is a journey of the self, through the self and ultimately for the self. Spiritual awakening is also referred as spiritual consciousness ( Pragyan or Adhyatma). It is the ultimate stage of learning.

**Spiritual consciousness (*pragyan* or *adhyatma*) :**

Knowledge of life, time, and space their beginning and end, have intrigued the mind of the scientific world, ever since the time of Archimedes, 288 B.C. The concept and theory of Science grew at a rapid pace post the 17$^{th}$ century known as the era of Isaac Newton after his observation of falling apple and the famous three laws of motion. Subsequently he developed the mechanistic view of the universe. It remained unchallenged for almost three hundred years. In the early 20$^{th}$ century, two remarkable theories changed the entire concept of the universe, life, and time. These were: one, Einstein's Theory of Relativity and second, the Theory of Quantum Mechanics. Science began to think and discover the 'God' particle as a fundamental building block of everything, from tiniest to the largest. The dilemma remains and the search continues. The statement and the firm belief that God exists is the premise of all religions. Science wants to establish the truth. Spiritualism starts on the premise of the truth.

The Hindu scriptures say:

*'Ekam Sat Vipra Bahudha Vadanti'*

Meaning: Truth is One, the wise call it by various names.

There is yet another verse:

*Eko aham Dwitiyo nasti,*

*Na bhooto na bhawishyati.*

Meaning: I (God) am one. There is no second. There was no one like me in the past nor will there be one in the future. I am eternal.

In Christianity, God is the Eternal Being who created and preserves all things.

In Islam, God (Allah), a contraction of *al-ilah* is the Absolute one and all-knowing ruler of the universe and the creator of everything.

From the above quotes we can see that the core concept of God is the same in all the major religions. The difference is in the means and method of self-realisation of God. The concept of self-realisation and the statements that, *Aham tatwam Asi* (I am within you) and *Aham Brahmasmi* (I am Brahma) is relevant only in Hinduism. We shall base our further elaboration on the Hindu scriptures, philosophy, and practice.

Over millenniums, we have had enlightened souls and sages from time-to-time who have experienced and revealed the ways to know the self, and through it, the Absolute. The ways were/are varied in nature. No matter which path one chooses the destination will be the same.

Some of the popular ways practised even today include:

- *Japa* (chanting of a mantra or prayer with a rosary)
- *Tapa* (a sort of meditation in total isolation)
- *Puja* (offering of flowers and sweets to the Gods and deities of faith)
- *Bhakti* (devotion with prayers and service to the God and Goddesses)
- *Karma* (right acts)
- *Gyan* (realisation of God through knowledge)

In almost all the above, **one thing is common - the neglect of the body to the point of starvation leading to emaciation.**

How these modes of practices evolved over time may be of interest in determining the path one opts for?

One of the units of time mentioned in the scriptures is a *yuga*. One *yuga* is 432,000 earthly years. There is mention of four Yugas based on their duration and quality (Guna) characteristics. These are:

1. *Satya yuga* lasts for 1,728,000 years.
2. *Treta yuga* lasts for 1,296,000 years.

3. *Dwapar yuga* lasts for 8,64,000 years.
4. *Kaliyuga* lasts for 432,000 years.

The four together make one *chaturyuga* of 4.32 million years. These are cyclical in nature and seamlessly transfer from one to the other. 1000 cycles of *chaturyugas* make a *kalpa*. A *kalpa* is 4.32 billion years, one day of Brahma.

Each *yuga* has been characterised by the *gunas* (pattern of moral and ethical behaviour) that will predominantly govern the conduct of the people in those times. Here are the brief descriptions:

*Satya yuga* will be a period with a white symbol. White is the symbol of purity. During this time, wisdom, self-control and equity will be seen everywhere. There will be no affliction of any kind.

In the *Treta yuga*, there will be a gradual increase in the desire for wealth and *kam* (sensual gratification) in the conduct of society. There will also be a gradual erosion of the white colour. A new culture of the desire of righteousness, wealth, and sense of gratification will evolve. This has been called *rajasi vritti*. It bears a red colour. There will be a mix of white and red during this era. A slow consistent rise of unethical behaviour and affliction from conflict will surface in society.

In the *Dwaper yuga*, there will be a further erosion of moral and ethical values. The white colour will shrink further, red will dominate and a new colour black will get space. Black signifies *tamasi vritti*.

*Tamasi* signifies vices like greed, jealousy, hatred, stealing, forceful possession, et cetera.

*Kaliyuga*, the time we are living in, will see 99 per cent erosion of truth and wisdom, little traces of *rajasi vritti*, and dominance of *tamasi vritti*. The period will have all kinds of physical, social, and natural afflictions of a disproportionate magnitude. Senses will rule over the mind and intelligence. Wealth will become the end and means to acquire power. Falsehood, favouritism, and nepotism will bring success and position. Sex will become the primary source of entertainment. As written by Dr S. Radhdakrishnan in *Kalki*, 'Money will walk, money will talk, when money speaks nothing interrupts.'

Spiritual pursuits in all these four yugas are briefly mentioned below. The add-on processes in each successive yuga can be well identified with the governing values and conduct of each period.

*Sat yuga* - Adopted the path of wisdom, *gyan* yoga

*Treta yuga* - Adopted the path of wisdom *gyan* plus *tapa* (penance)

*Dwapar yuga* - Adopted the path of *gyan*, *tapa*, *bhakti* (devotion), *puja* (worship) and *karma*

*Kaliyuga* - Adopted all from *dwapar* but only as deceit and deception to earn wealth. There is great emphasis on idol worship and rituals for self-gains.

Sage Patanjali (500-200 B.C.) presumed to be the incarnation of *Adishesh*, the couch for Lord Vishnu, could visualise the problems with *japa*, *tapa*, *gyan*, and *puja* where the physical well-being was always at the receiving end. He came out with his concept of *Astha Yoga* through which one could strengthen one's physical, mental abilities, alertness and well control the life energies.

These eight petals of Patanjali yoga have been defined in 194 aphorisms. These are also known as *Patanjali Yoga Sutras*.

The eight petals or formats of *Patanjali Astha Yoga* are:

- *Yama*
- *Niyam*
- *Asana*
- *Pranayam*
- *Pratyahar*
- *Dharana* (concentration)
- *Dhyan* (meditation)
- *Samadhi* (deep and uninterrupted meditation)

A detailed explanation of these is provided in the chapters that follow. The important thing that must be underlined here is that the first four of *Patanjali Astha Yoga*, that is, *yama*, *niyam*, *asana*, and *pranayam* focus on a healthy, firm, flexible, lustring body, and a very robust immune system with high energy levels. **That is the most striking reason why**

**yoga is different! Its priority is a healthy body and a robust system.**

There are some misgivings about yoga too. Yoga getting popular by the day is a promising thing. However, if practised in a wrong fashion it can be harmful too. It must be noted that yoga:

- Is relaxation. It is not to cause fatigue, discomfort or unnatural pain at any stage.
- Is never a mass activity. It is best done alone in a serene environment.
- Laziness is its enemy.
- Proceed gradually and systematically.

Finally, no amount of reading and discussion will be able to bring the benefit including the realisation of the truth. Follow the chosen path regularly and with total commitment. The road must be walked by you alone. No one will walk it for you.

# PATANJALI'S ASHTHA (EIGHT LIMBS) OF YOGA

In the preceding chapter on why 'yoga is different', there was a reference to *Patanjali Ashtha Yoga* (often called the eight petals or stages of *Patanjali Yoga*). The essence of this has been explained through 196 aphorisms. These aphorisms are mostly one-liners. The first aphorism reads:

*Atha Yoga Anushashnam*

Meaning: Yoga is discipline.

Second aphorism:

*Chitti vritti Nirodhah*

Meaning: Yoga is the cessation of thoughts.

These aphorisms are known as *sutras*. *Sutra* in Sanskrit is a kind of compressed narrative. It is easy to remember. These Sutras are like a beacon for the practitioner. It eases the navigation. Those who take the guidance with commitment will be in a direction to the destination. We shall try to expand and elaborate these sutras in subsequent chapters.

But first, a brief introduction to the cause and purpose of Patanjali's appearance on planet earth.

In time reckoning, the Patanjali period lasted from 500 to 200 BC. There is an interesting anecdote about his birth. In Hindu mythology, Patanjali, in his earlier life was Sheshnag (King of Serpents) and served as a couch to Lord Vishnu, one of the trinity Godheads (Brahma, Vishnu, and Mahesh). Shiva is one of the many names of Mahesh. Shiva, amongst his many divine acts, is also known for the *Tandava Nritya* (a kind of dance). It is believed that he performs this dance when in a euphoric state of happiness. It also symbolises His anger and the destruction it causes. Once, Shiva was in a blissful state and was performing His famous Tandav dance amidst the gathering of the Gods. During this period, Sheshnag was uncomfortable due to the expanding form and increasing body weight of his master, Lord Vishnu. Towards the end, the weight became unbearable. Fortunately at that moment Lord Shiva concluded His dance and the form and body weight of Lord Vihnu became normal.

After some time the Sheshnag sought permission from his master and enquired the secret of his expanding form and increasing body weight. Lord Vishnu explained that it was due to the intensity of energy generated from the sound of the dance. Sheshnag could not comprehend this logic. The curiosity enhanced. Why could he not feel the same? Upon his insistence, Lord Vishnu told him that to experience it he would need to get into the human form which could be possible with the blessings of Lord Shiva. With the blessings of Lord Shiva, Adishesha appeared on planet earth. He was nourished and raised by a pious lady named Gonica.

Gonica was a pious lady with great erudition and knowledge of the Hindu scriptures. She had no child. In her old age, she was lonely and was occasionally filled with remorse. She wanted to pass on her experience and wisdom to someone worthy of it. One fine morning, after a bath in the river, as she was offering oblation to god Surya (Sun God) a tiny fish with a human head and voice fell in her folded palms.

The fish addressed her as a mother and begged not to be put back in the river. Gonica accepted the request, adopted him as her son and named him Patanjali (*Pat* in Hindi means to fall, *Anjali* is the shape of the open palms put together. This shape enables the collection of holy water in the palms) - the fish that fell (pat) in her anjali derives the name Patanjali.

Patanjali wrote three invaluable books for the benefit of humankind. These were:

- -*Maha Bhasya* (a book on language and communication)
- *Ayurved* (Medicine and Health)

- *-Yoga Darshan* (knowledge of the absolute through knowledge of the self). The book provides an unparallel account of the art and science of yoga. It gave birth to the now-famous *Patanjali Astha Yoga*. This forms the principal subject matter of what follows.

## Patanjali Astha Yoga

Patanjali identified two great impediments in the physical or spiritual progress of human beings.

- Physical afflictions
- A fleeting and unsteady mind

Patanjali's entire work on yoga is focused on control, mitigation and finally, freedom of the human body from all kind of afflictions. The process and methodologies are systematically covered under eight stages. Each stage prepares one to usher into the next. One weakness we often suffer from is our keenness to know the endpoint without experiencing the intermediate points. This is discouraged in any endeavour and in yoga it is prohibited.

We shall now try to understand each of the eight stages separately. It must be reiterated that the separation is only from the viewpoint of understanding. In reality, these are all intertwined. Each stage prepares the practitioner for the next stage.

The eight limbs or stages are:

1. *Yama* (principles of life-ethical conduct).

2. *Niyam* (social etiquette and behaviour-moral conduct).

3. *Asana* (various postures of the body).

4. *Pranayam* (the art and science of breathing).

5. *Pratyahar* (control of the senses).

6. *Dharna* (concentration).

7. *Dhyan* (meditation).

8. *Samadhi* (uninterrupted prolonged meditation).

Of the eight stages, the first four can be grouped together. These four -*Yama*, *Niyam*, *Asana*, and *Pranayam* provide robustness, flexibility, and firmness to the body. These also initiate control of the mind through controlled breathing. Persistent and regular practice of these four petals of yoga bestows upon the practitioner the much-needed discipline, strength, stamina, and poise. Thus, the practitioner is well-equipped to practice and experience the higher and subtler stages of yoga.

## Purpose of Each Stage of Yoga:

## Yama

'*Ahimsa, satya, asteya,*

*Brahmacharya, aparigrah, yamah.* '

Non-violence, truthfulness, non-stealing,

Celibacy or continence, non-covetousness.

This is the self-discipline one needs to adopt as a core principle in personal lif

What is cause to an effect is means to an end. We often hear in general conversation, 'do not use a hammer to kill a fly.' The message it conveys is that the choice of means and its intensity of application should be commensurate to the desired end. Humans, because they have reasoning power, are argumentative. Such arguments may involve ideas and ideologies, business strategies, property, and asset sharing, etc. Peaceful arguments grow into heated discussions. Failure to reach a peaceful resolution leads to rivalry and conflict. Small matters become big stakes. Wars have been fought to proclaim victory. Often principle of, 'might is right' prevails over a peaceful resolution.

Within us, we are a mix of conflicts; we argue and we fight within. Our complex nature gives rise to reason versus emotion, hate versus love, compassion versus jealousy, ego versus acceptance, and possession versus renunciation. We can add more to it. We have such fascinating arguments as death versus life. Is death the end of life? Or is death the beginning of a new life? Is there life after death? Answers to these questions are not easy. The true answer can never be obtained through arguments. The only way is through yogic practices. The senses can be controlled through yoga. The mind can be stilled, the self can be discovered and the absolute can be realised. The journey is individual. The path is pathless. Experiences can vary depending on the intensity and endurance of the practitioner but the destination remains the same. The experience will be non-verbal and non-transferable. The means will always be peaceful and non-violent (*Ahimsa*) free from all dualities. Therefore, the path of yoga is the path of salvation through peace and Ahimsa. Each word, associated explanation and related action has to be understood in the true spirit and practised with full dedication. The first in the process is the correct interpretation of the words and the Sutras to be followed by their application in our routine life. So, let us begin with the understanding of the words used to form the Sutras.

*Ahimsa*, as defined by Patanjali is:

*'Ahimsa pratishthayam tat sanidhau vaira tyagah.'*

Patanjali. Sutra 35.

Ahimsa: non-violence, one that does not hurt.

Pratisthayam: something well-established within; something that has become one's nature.

Tat: his or her.

Sanidhau: in close proximity, company.

Vaira: enmity.

Tyagah: abandon, get rid of.

Meaning: Aura around a person totally established*
in the principle of non-violence will be peaceful.
The proximity of such a person will convert even
creatures with ferocious nature into a state of non-violence and peace.

* Refers to one who is non-violent in words,
thoughts, and actions. Such a person is presumed
to have conquered vices like hate, jealousy, and
anger.

## Truthfulness

Once, Mahatma Gandhi, whom the world knows
as a great practitioner of *satya* (truth) and an apostle
of peace and non-violence (*ahimsa*), was asked,
'What is the most difficult thing to practice?'
Gandhiji replied, 'To speak the truth.'

A follow-up question was, 'What is the easiest thing
to practice?' His response was, 'To speak the truth.'

Indeed, the easiest and most beautiful thing to
practice in life is the adoption of truthfulness. One
who practices it will only speak the truth or what
such a person speaks will be considered the truth.
But as Gandhiji said, 'It is not an easy task to adapt
and live with truthfulness.' Let us examine the yogic
interpretation as stated by Patanjali.

*'Satyapratisthayam kriya phalahasrayatvam.'*

Patanjali. Sutra 36.

*Satya*: truth.

*Pratisthayam*: fully established, becoming part of nature.

*Kriya*: to act.

*Phalah*: gain, result, benefit.

*Asrayatvam*: *asraya* is to support, foundation.

The literal translation is: All acts of a person firmly established in truth will be built on a foundation that will be beneficial to all.

The true measure of truthfulness is not merely limited to expression, action, and the resultant outcome (*phal*). The awareness of truthfulness should percolate to each living cell of the body (we have 37 trillion of them). Each cell must feel the vibe and purity of the truth. One who can attain this state of conscious awareness about the truth will experience an abode of divinity in thoughts, words, and actions. The spoken or unspoken wishes of such a person will always be fulfilled.

## Asteya (Non-stealing)

Stealing though undesirable is tempting. Sometimes it is need based but mostly it is greed driven. When desires cannot be fulfilled with available resources stealing appears a tempting option. It is not limited to material wealth alone: we steal ideas, we spy stealthily, we invade into someone's privacy. In short, all acts that cannot be disclosed in public fall in the category of stealing. Further, all acts that the conscience does not approve of, be it ethical, moral or religious, fall under the category of stealing.

What is the way to stop stealing? The social stigma attached to it is of little significance. Punitive measures as a deterrent do have some impact, but the evil exists. In the world of yoga, the focus is on thought control. It aims to delete the word stealing from the thought circuit. After all, it is thought that triggers action. Is it possible to control or dummy such thoughts? In yoga, denial of desires and thought control forms a part of *Pratyahar*. This has been discussed in detail under the title, *Pratyahar*, which is the fifth stage of *Astha Yoga*. For the moment, let us evaluate the concerned sutra on non-stealing.

*'Asteya pratisthayam sarva ratno upasthanam.'*

Patanjali. Sutra 37.

*Asteya*: non-stealing.

*Pratisthayam*: To be fully established in. To become part of nature.

*Sarva*: total, all

*Ratno*: precious stone, gems.

*Upasthanam*: accessible, in possession of.

The literal meaning of the *sutra* is: one who is fully established in the concept of *Asteya*, is (by implication) a rich man.

In our daily lives, we observe people to whom little is more. We also see those whom more is without boundary, an insatiable desire. It can be seen as a function of contentment versus discontentment. This desire of more without boundary may stimulate to work hard or expand the work domain. It may also lead to unethical means of earning. The constant and devoted practice of yoga delivers one from such acts. With awareness, non-stealing becomes a part of nature. The idea looks simple; the senses generate a desire, the desire triggers the mind, the mind initiates action, yoga controls the mind through awareness and the desire is denied, the temptation to steal vanishes, contentment sets in. With conscious practice non-stealing becomes a part of nature. In the initial stage it may be a mere act and might cause a certain degree of discomfort. When it forms a part of nature it renders joy and happiness.

## Celibate (Brahmacharya)

### Who is a Celibate?

Sex organs in the male and female bodies are classified as one of the *Karmendriyas* (senses of action). It is through the interaction of these that reproduction takes place. Different species have different reproduction process and cycles. There are single-cell organisms where the cells divide into two and the chain multiplies. There are insects with combined characteristics of the male and female. In the case of humans, the semen of the male body combines with the egg/ova of the female body to form a life. In case of humans sexual act and reproduction has acquired a specialised scientific approach in compared to lower forms of life.

Through science or traditional wisdom semen and sperm are considered vital energy. These form the essence of life. Well preserved semen and sperm provide energy, grace and brilliance to the body. It improves memory, strength and endurance. Brahmacharya, act of sexual continence, is therefore highly desirable during the student or learning period of life which, in Hindu tradition, is considered to be the first 25 years of one's life. On the contrary excessive sexual indulgence is inimical to good health. It can cause avoidable affliction and even accelerate the process of life's end. It is normally considered that the one who abstains from sexual relations is a celibate. A celibate possesses the brilliance of knowledge and energy.

Questions are often asked about the rationale of celibacy. Traditional religious practices prohibit marriage and sex for yogis and monks. In ancient Hindu traditions there are instances of sages getting married and having reared children. Sages like Vashishtha and Vishwamitra are some of the names often quoted. Both had attained the highest rank and recognition in the yogic hierarchy and were married. The available explanation is that responsible and selective sex together with chastity at the right time and duration can be accepted as celibacy. The advantage and efficacy of sexual abstinence are well recognised in yogic life. It is equally considered a virtue in normal life. However, love, lust, and sex are irresistible endowments to all living entities. This may be the reason for a more lenient and permissive view in different faiths and communities. Marriage traditions of one man to one woman, polygamy to polyandry, and sex outside matrimony are evidence of a wide acceptance of sexual conduct. The advantage of abstinence is immense but the urge to enact is more a matter of self discipline than social, religious or legal sanction. Therefore, let us live with the more manageable concept of responsible and selective sex and chastity.

## Sex Energy in Yoga.

Regular and proper practice of yoga enhances the ability to have prolonged and intense sex. However, there are references of acquisition of high intensity sex energy through yoga, also referred as *Ashwa Shakti* (horsepower). Anyone endowed with this level of sex energy needs to exercise great self control. Indiscriminate and frequent, prolonged sex may harm the partner.

We have seen the liberal view on sex and the rationale for it. However, in the first 25 years of life, the liberal view is not applicable. This period is generally marked for learning and skill development necessary to further the cause and purpose of life. Sex is considered a great distraction and hindrance in learning. Sex in any form, including the thought process or casual discussion, is discouraged during this period. Perhaps keeping this in mind the initial 25 years of life has been identified as "Student Life'- period to study and learn.

*'Brahmcharya pratishthayam virya labhah'.*

Patanjali, Sutra 38.

*Brahmacharya*: Celibate, chastity.

*Pratisthayam*: Fully established.

*Virya*: Energy and vigour.

*Labhah*: Gain, benefit.

Meaning: One who is fully established in continence will be full with energy and vigour.

Sexual energy is the strongest manifestation of life force and romantic love. The meeting of the egg and sperm is not just a physical phenomenon. It carries with it the passion and emotion of the *Purusha* (the man) and *Prakriti* (the woman) that gives birth to a life.

For a true yogi, sex and celibacy are the *sadhana* of a high order. The *Vedas* say:

*'Brahmacharyena tapsa deva mrityu upadhanat.'*

(Meaning: Through the practice of *Brahmacharya* the Gods conquered death and attained *Brahma* -the Supreme salvation, *Brahma Lin* status.)

## Aparigrah (non-covetousness)

The literal meaning of *Aparigrah* is the reluctance to accept material obligations;

-Refusal to donation,

- Limit possession essential for survival alone.

- Increasing loss of interest in the material world and -    - Renunciation.

According to Patanjali, the one who is completely established into this act can know the secret of life, its past and the future.

*'Aparigrah yastharya janm kathaant sambodhah.'*

Patanjali, Sutra 39.

*Aparigraha*: minimum or no possession.

*Sthairye*: stable, fully committed to.

*Janma*: birth, life.

*Kathamta*: process, details.

*Sambodhah*: awareness, knowledge.

A person, detached from material possessions and bondage thereto will know the process (secret) of the past and future lives.

When non-possessiveness becomes a part of nature it does not relate only to material objects. Not holding rigidly to one's thoughts is also a characteristic of such a person. A clairvoyant- one who can see through time- will appreciate the essence of flexible ideas.

*Aparigrah* is the subtlest of all the *Yamas*. It is difficult too. It reveals the purpose of this life and beyond.

## Niyam

We shall now move to the second of the eight stages, i.e., *Niyam* (conduct to follow, strengthening of self discipline).

*'souch santosh tapah swadhyaya iswarpranidhanani niyamah.'*

*Souch*: means cleanliness.

*Santosh*: means contentment.

*Tapa*: means total surrender to the cause undertaken.

*Swadhyaya*: means study of the self in its every aspect.

*Iswarpranidhan*: means total faith in God.

All interactive social and ethical principles are dynamic in nature. These are therefore subject to change and adjustments. Amid these dynamics there exist some principles which, if adhered to, will make an individual and the social ecosystem more liveable and pleasurable. Patanjali has defined these as:

- Cleanliness.
- Contentment.
- Religious austerity, tenacity.
- *Swadhyaya*, study and knowledge of the self.
- *Iswarpranidhan*, devotion to God, total submission.

These are self explaining. Yet, let us try to expand the meaning and effect of these in yoga perspective.

## Cleanliness (Sauchat)

In the chapter titled, 'Why is Yoga Different,' there is a mention that unlike other modes of spiritual pursuit yoga places high priority on the healthy body. In yoga, a firm and healthy body forms the pedestal on which the total spiritual architecture is designed and constructed. Cleanliness of the body is one such element.

*sauchat svangajugupsa paraih asamsargah*

Patanjali Sutra 40.

*Sauchat*: means cleanliness, freshness, purity.

*Sva*: means self.

*Anga*: means the limbs, the body.

*Jugupsa*: means aversion, keep a distance.

*Paraih*: means others.

*Asamsargah*: means no physical contact whatsoever.

The intent of the above *sutra* is that a clean and pure body-mind system is averse to physical contact with another person. This also implies contacts related to sensual gratification.

In yoga, the body is considered a temple, housing the soul. The body has its intelligence and intellect. Cleanliness of the body is not merely physical. It includes physiological and intellectual purity too. A clean and pure body-mind combination helps the practitioner control sensual desires. When sensual desires are under control the mind is free to focus on the inner self, awareness intensifies, the joy of knowing, and understanding the self, its nature, and grace dawns. Path to the spiritual journey gets clearer.

## Santosh (Contentment)

We have observed that bathing and cleaning of our body is an essential daily routine. Bathing is an energy provider. It makes the senses fresh and sharp. There is an element of purity felt within. What will be the state of realisation when we bathe all our senses, inner organs and thoughts in the same way as the body? Sure enough, it will add to the strength, desire, and resolve of the practitioner to follow the chosen path.

*Santosat anuttamah sukh labhah*

Patanjali, Sutra 42.

*Santosat*: means from contentment.

*Anuttamah*: means excellent, without a match, supreme.

*Sukh*: means happiness.

*Labhah*: means gain, benefit.

Meaning: From supreme contentment comes supreme happiness.

Supreme contentment here refers to the controlled desire and awakened consciousness.

## Tapa (religious austerity, tenacity, an act of avowed commitment)

*Tapa* is an avowed act of self-discipline. Tapa destroys the impurities of thoughts and senses. One who follows all the *Yam* (*Ahimsa*, *Satya*, *Brahmacharya*, *Asteya* and *Aparigrah*) and *Niyam* (such as, *Sauch* and *Santosh*) with determination develops the desire to *Swadhyaya* (the study of self) and *Iswarpranidhan* (a total devotion to God). Some equate *Tapa* to penance. It means deliberate infliction of suffering through deprivation, including starvation. In yoga, *Tapa* is purely a committed discipline with no relation to suffering.

*kaya indriya siddhih asuddhiksayat tapasah*

                                          Patanjali. Sutra 43.

*Kaya*: means body.

*Indriya*: means senses.

*Siddhih*: means attainment, success.

*Ksayat*: means destruction, disappearance.

Meaning: Through *Tapa* (dedicated discipline), the body and the senses are purified. All impurities of thought, perception and action are destroyed.

The practitioner is now on the right path, appropriately equipped to move forward to attain the spiritual goal.

## Swadhyaya

*Swa* means 'self' and *adhyaya* refers to 'study.' Invariably we err in defining the purpose and meaning of this all-important word. It is construed as an act of self-study. Ironically it is the wrong interpretation. It means the **study of the self**. A systematic study of the gross body to the most subtle of the constituent- consciousness- is *Swadhaya*. It is a journey from out to in, from the seeker to the seer and vice-versa. The practitioner becomes aware of all functions of the body components. Through this kind of awareness, vision and goal become transparent and clear.

*Swadhyayat istadevata samprayogah.*

Patanjali. Sutra 44.

*Swadhyayat*: means the study of the self. Some equate it to a parallel study of the scriptures.

*Istadevata*: means the God one worships or has faith in.

*Samprayogah*: means to be in communion.

The *sutra* literally translated will mean:

Knowledge of the self leads to the knowledge of the God.

## Ishwarpranidhan

*Ishwarpranidhan* is a total surrender to God. It demands an unreserved faith in the existence of God and His grace. There are some who want a proof of His existence, His abode and His expanse. This is an interesting, amusing and a critical relationship between the Creator and His most intelligent creation, humans. Those few who have the answer are not capable of sharing nor transferring or showing it in any tangible form. Knowledge has four primary sources.

1. Self-experience.
2. Conjecture or presumption, a logical approach.
3. Experiment, scientific approach.
4. Metaphysics, the evolution of the philosophy of life and the universe.

Seekers of the truth can fall into two categories: one with the total faith in God and the others with doubt in His existence. Both can follow the principles of yoga. The one with faith will begin at stage one. Others will start with two, three and four before returning to one. I leave the merit of the two options to be judged by the reader.

The realisation of God is through self-experience. *Patanjali Astha Yoga* lays down a very systematic step-by-step method to come face-to-face with the Absolute Truth of God realisation. The Theory of Dualism is the basis of knowledge evolution. We either accept a theory and prove its veracity or deny a theory in the absence of a tangible and acceptable proof. In both the cases we apply all the talents and tools at our disposal to reach the desired conclusion. In yoga the practitioner can only share his experience. He is the enquirer. He is also the facilitator and provider of all the tools. All the basic elements needed for the experiment are within. He can elaborate on the process and procedures he followed. He can share his landmark experiences. And if he has experienced the Ultimate can he share it? That is biggest dilemma in spiritual world. He himself has attained the ultimate goal and is free from any duality. He can with peace and poise say, **'EKO AHAM DWITIYO NASTI'**. He can assert Omnipresent and Omnipotent nature of God. But will it satisfy those who are looking for a more tangible proof. Here is the answer provided by Sant Kabir, the great saint and poet of 16th century.

'Kabira bat agamya ki,

Kahan sunan ki nahi,

Jo janat so kahat nahi,

kahat so janat nahi.'

(Contextual meaning: The Unknowable cannot be known through discourse and dialogue. One who knows (Him) will not be able to describe His true nature and His expanse. One who tries to elaborate upon Him does not know His true nature.)

He is the Cause of all. At Him everything ends. This has been succinctly and effectively narrated by Lord Krishna when He uttered the following verse (*shloka*) to Arjuna:

*Sarvadharman paritajya mam ekam sharnam brajah,*

*Aham twa sarva papebhayah mokshashyami ma suchah.*

Bhagawad Gita, verse 66, ch. 18.

*Sarvadharman*: means all your acts righteously done.

*Paritajya*: means to renounce.

*Mam*: means me.

*Ekam*: means only (emphasis on the word '*mam ekam*,' Me only, Me alone).

*Sharanam braj*: means to take refuge.

*Aham*: means I, Me.

*Twa*: means you.

*Sarvapapebhaya*: means all the acts of sin.

*Mokshaashyami*: means to absolve.

*Ma Suchah*: means need not worry.

Meaning: Renounce all your acts and achievements. Surrender unto Me and Me alone. I shall absolve you of all your sins and grant *Moksha*, salvation.

In life big and small achievements remain engrained in memory. These memories keep the ego and existence of 'I' alive. By renouncing these one becomes free from ego. Essentially, neither the acts nor the achievements were ever yours. The last of the Patanjali aphorism, *sutra* 196, conveys an almost similar message. It reads:

*Purushartha sunyanam, gunanam pratiprasavah,*

*Kaivalyam Swarup pratisthava chittisakti iti.*

The sutra defines that the state of *Kaivalya*, total liberation is possible only when one has freed the mind of all acts, achievements, and all *gunas* (refers to all kind of thoughts, desires, and emotions that drive action).

In our life of physical existence such statements are considered mythological or spiritual in nature, beyond the need and scope of normal worldly life. To many these are a sort of storytelling exercises. The elders in the family narrate and the young ones listen in mere courtesy or curiosity. The youth and the middle age and those on the margin of being called seniors have little time or patience for such philosophy, principle or practice. They are not wrong either. They have to perform their worldly responsibilities related to each stage of physical life;

infancy stage to baby stage, to childhood, to adolescent, to youth, mid age to old age.

Each stage has its own goal. Each stage also evolves the individual ability to achieve his/her life's goal. The spiritual masters classified physical life cycle in four principal phases and the principal goal of each phase. In time frame each phase is assigned 25 years (from a total of 100 years assumed human longevity)progressively counted from birth to nirvana in sequence stated below;

1. *Vidhyarthi jeevan. First 25 years of life.* (student or learning phase). Meant to be devoted to learning and acquisition of skill.
2. *Grahastha jeevan. 26to 50 years.* (sense gratification and earning phase ).
3. *Vanprastha jeevan. 51 to 75 years.* Phase of life to share experience and process to pass on the skill and responsibilities to generation next. Beginning of a natural shift to charity, hope, love and faith.
4. *Sanyas jeevan* (life of renunciation) 76th. year onwards. Devoted in pursuit of spiritual knowledge. Realisation of self and the Supreme.

*Transiting from one stage to the other is not easy. Principle and practice of Yoga becomes a natural ally to facilitate the transformation from one phase to the other. We shall try to see how yoga relates these phases with related duties and responsibilities. Yoga philosophy sets four principal goals of human life, Dharma, Artha, Kam, Moksha.*

*Dharma:* (Study of righteousness in our actions).

- *Artha:* (application of skill and work to earn Position, power, wealth and fame).
- *Kam:* (gratification of senses and procreation).
- *Moksha:* (spiritual pursuit, search for salvation).

We shall try to see how practice of yoga will help in realisation of these goals.

To a devoted practitioner yoga provides a robust body, strong memory and creative mind. It enables the individual to be more focussed and at peace with himself and his work environment. His joy of material world will be free from greed, jealousy and hatred. His presence will bring in an aura of faith, commitment and goodwill. It will greatly enhance the ability to Artha and Kam aspects of life.

Practice of yoga, especially those who reach the stage of Pratyahar, causes increasing loss of interest in the material world. Such a person becomes, 'karm mukta'. His sole devotion will be on the work not on its benefits. This will be beneficial in disengagement from the material world and transition to the Spiritual world.

Those seeking the Truth in the spiritual world will find the philosophy of yoga as useful tool and the technique to facilitate the journey to destination. We shall try to devote a little more space and time to this aspect of life.

For the faithful, God is the Truth. To the scientific world, God is Cosmic Consciousness. Yet to others, God is the all-pervading energy. Whatever the name and faith or belief one possesses, Truth is One. Everything else is part of that One. Everything is borne of Him. At the end, everything ends in Him.

"*Ekam sat vipra bahudha vadanti*,

    Rig ved Samhita, 1.164.46

The above verse from the rg ved means: Truth is one. The wise call me by different names.

An episode from *Mahabharata* will be worth mentioning here. There is a character with the name Barbarika. He was the grandchild of Bheem. Barbarika's father was Ghatotkach. Barbarika was a brave warrior. He was blessed to be unconquerable. However, he had made a promise to his *Guru* (teacher). The promise was that in times of need he would always fight in favour of the weak. This put the Pandvas, whose progeny he was, in a quandary. It meant that he was free to change sides with the changing dynamics of the war and therefore, the victory of any side could not be guaranteed. In the absence of any plausible solution Lord Krishna, who was the protector of the Pandvas and upholder of Dharma, had to step in.

He felt that the only way to ensure the victory of the Pandvas was to disallow Barbrika from participating in the ensuing war. The Lord asked Barbarika to donate to Him his dismembered head as a mark of *guru dakshina* (an established obligation that a disciple or guardian was obliged to honour after the completion of formal schooling and in accordance with the demand of the teacher. Krishna had taught Barbarika in his early stages but had not accepted the guru dakshina). Apparently, it was a gruesome demand. Everyone was stunned. Barbarika beheaded himself. On the advice of Krishna the severed head was placed at a height commanding the battlefield. His dismembered body was safely preserved. Barbarika was blessed that he would be able to witness the epic war with full awareness from beginning till end. At the end of the war, the victorious side of the Pandavas and Lord Krishna visited Barbarika. His life was restored. He was asked to describe what all did he see in the war of Mahabharata. He replied, **"Everywhere and in everything, I saw only Krishna."**

That explains the earlier assertion, 'I am the cause of everything. Everything ends at me.'

*Iswarpranidhan* is the total acceptance in the Supreme Power and Nature of God.

Simply explained it means everything is part of the one Supreme Consciousness. Its easiest realisation is through unflinching, single minded faith, Ishwarpranidhan.

## Asana

*Sthir sukham asnam*

Patanjali, sutra 46.

*Sthir* is firm

*Sukham* means one rendering comfort

*Asanam* means an act of posturing

*Asan* renders firmness to the body and makes it comfortable to live with.

What is *Asana*?

The slow, but steady movement of various parts of the body from its normal position to a different position, to hold oneself in the altered posture for a reasonable time before returning to the original position, can be called an Asana in motion. Repetition of such acts delivers physical benefits to the body parts involved, and to the entire body structure as well.

In all there are two hundred *asanas*, from simple standing, sitting, sleeping, headstand to difficult ones like bending, twisting, curling or other distorted shapes. Each one of these provides firmness and flexibility to the body. In certain cases these also provide therapeutic value to minor/major ailments. These can also be useful in fast health recovery process post major medical procedures. Below we shall try to introduce some of the easy –to-do asanas that all age groups with no severe health problems can do on a routine basis. But first, let us understand the ten golden rules of asanas. In fact, many of these are applicable to yoga in general.

## Ten Golden Rules while doing Asanas/Yoga.

1. All movements must be slow and steady.

2. All movements must be against resistance. In majority of the cases the resistance is self-generated. In exceptional cases external resistance through added weight and spring attachments can be applied under proper supervision.

3. At no stage shall the individual continue with unease and discomfort except the stress of stretches and natural incidental aches and pain.

4. In a state of fatigue and unbearable, unnatural discomfort the *asana* should be stopped and guidance sought.

5. All *asanas* have to be done on an empty stomach and an empty bladder.

6. The choice of place and timing should be retained as far as possible.

7. Open-air should be preferred over a closed conditioned environment (not a must condition).

8. Always keep a glass of water handy to be taken at the end of the session or when needed. Also keep a wet hand towel for excess saliva or phlegm disposal.

9. Most important: Try to synchronise the movement with the breath. Under no situation or posture, one should hold breath unless it is a part of the *asana*.

10. Remember, yoga is never an exercise to cause exhaustion or exertion. In the end, it is always a relaxation. It brings comfort, grace, and beauty to the gross and subtle bodies.

Finally, it provides the practitioner with physical firmness, flexibility, and strength to accomplish his onward journey with comfort, efficiency, and commitment. Physical fitness is the pre-requisite for success and happiness in the world of phenomenon. It is equally important for success in the spiritual world.

## Some easy –to-do asanas.

As mentioned earlier there are nearly two hundred asanas. In fact any conscious change in physical posture from normal can be termed as asana. This includes laughing, yawning to simple stretching. The qualifying condition is that the act should be consciously done with a pre-determined objective.

We shall briefly deal with some of the most doable *asanas* and their benefits.

## 1. TADASANA (mountain pose)

It is an *asana* that everyone can possibly do and benefit from.

-Stand straight on a firm clean surface with feet parallel and together. In case you find it difficult to balance, create a space between the feet of not more than 8 to 10 cm.

-Press the heels and toes down. Stretch the legs upward. Ensure that the feet remain firmly grounded and do not change their orientation.

-Tighten the knees and the thigh muscles by pulling them upwards.

-Create stress on the hips and the buttocks by pulling them inwards and up.

-The torso, the head, and the spine shall be stretched as a unit.

-Hands stretched on sides facing inside and touching the thighs.

-Continue with prolonged silent breathing.

-Maintain this posture for 30 seconds and progressively increase to 60 seconds.

-Relax for 10 -15 seconds.

-Repeat the cycle 10 times. Those finding it hard in one go can fragment it into two or three stages.

-Relax.

If there is nothing else to do go into *Savasan* (dead pose) for 10-20 minutes.

Sit straight and have a glass of water. Feel and follow the passage as the water gently flows into the system.

## Benefits other than feel good.

**This *asana* regularly done teaches the art of balanced and straight standing. It assists in keeping the body posture correct and the spine straight. It tones all the leg muscles including the hips and the buttocks. It also controls age-related degeneration of these muscles and the spine. It is good for people with knee problems.**

**Tadasana is a prelude to all asanas done in a standing posture.**

**Variants to Tadasana**

**1a.** *Tadasana* with hands down , fingers pointing down, palms 30 cm away from the body, relaxed face, drawn-in stomach, bodyweight equally distributed on both legs, abdomen tucked in and all muscles and the spine stretched, conscious normal breath. Remain in this posture for 30 seconds and progressively increase to 60 seconds. Return to normal and relax.

Repeat ten times. Further actions as advised under 1.

**1b. *Tadasana* with fingers interlocked:** In this pose, the practitioner needs to follow the instructions as under 1 above (under *Tadasana*), except that the palms are over the head, facing upwards with fingers interlocked. Rest of the acts are exactly as explained under *Tadasana*, except pull in the stomach and lift the sternum. With conscious breathing, remain in this position for 30 seconds, and progressively increase to 60 seconds. Return to normal position. Relax 10 to 15 seconds. Repeat the cycle 10 times. If found hard one can fragment it into stages.

If nothing further to do, go to *Savasana* and follow details as under *Tadasana*.

## 2. Forward bend (UTTANASANA)

-Stand firmly as in *Tadasana*.

-Legs to be fully stretched.

-Torso, including the head, to be considered one unit.

-Bodyweight to be equally distributed on both legs.

-Raise hands with palms open and facing outwards.

-Take a deep breath in.

-Bend slowly forward from the hip together with the hand.

-Bend to the point possible.

-During forward bending, breathe out.

-Retain the posture for 10 seconds. One can progressively increase the duration.

-During this period, keep breathing.

-At no stage should the legs bend. The leg muscles shall remain stretched throughout.

-Return to the original position while breathing in.

-Relax for 10-15 seconds.

-Repeat the process 10 times.

-If nothing else to, do go into *Savasan* (dead pose) for 10/20 minutes.

-Sit straight and take a glass of water with the full realisation of its passage and flow into the system.

**Note: Not recommended for those with a spinal disc problem. On the other hand, it relieves abdominal and back pains and tones the liver and kidneys.**

## 3. Backward Bending

All steps under forward bending will be applied to backward bending. The difference will be in the positioning of the arms. Here is a quick revision of the steps to be taken:

-Stand straight and firm with feet together.

-Legs, thighs, and hip muscles stretched and pulled up. Buttocks pulled in.

- Take the hands to the rear side. Interlock the fingers. Stretch the hands.

- The torso and the head are to move as one unit. The spine should remain as straight as possible.

- Bodyweight to be equally distributed on both legs.

- Take a deep breath in. Slowly and steadily, bend backward with slow exhalation.

- Bend to the point possible without causing pain other than the stress of stretch.

- Remain in that position for 10 seconds.

- Slowly return to the original position with breath in.

- Relax for 10-15 seconds.

- Repeat the cycle 5 times, can be extended as practice advances.

- Relax.

If nothing else to, do go into *Savasan* position as explained and follow routine.

This *asana* is extremely beneficial to stop back pain. It also provides flexibility to the spine. Remember, firmness and flexibility is the essence of *asanas*.

## 4. Dandasana

Just as *Tadasana* is the key to all other standing asanas, *Dandasana* is the key to all sitting asanas.

These include the forward and backward bends and the various twists.

*Dandasana* is basically a sitting posture with legs stretched forward. With the practice of this, one gets into the habit of sitting straight with an erect spine. It is highly beneficial against back pain common in persons spending long hours sitting on chairs.

**Procedure:**

Accessories required: One thin blanket or sheet, two brick size blocks with a smooth edge and surface.

-Choose a plane, hard clean surface. It can be the floor with a rubber mat or a flatbed with wooden planks (called *chowkee* in Hindi).

-Sit on the folded blanket or sheet with legs fully stretched forward.

-The spine shall be as erect as possible and firmly held in that posture throughout the asana.

-You will sit on the bones across the anus. Never sit on the bums.

-Place the blocks on the sides in line with the shoulders and parallel to the thighs.

- Place the palms on the blocks.

-Use the hands to pull the muscles of the buttocks out on both sides to ensure that the weight is on the buttock bones.

-Keep the legs from feet to thighs straight and fully stretched.

-Bring the hands down with palms pressing on the surface and the elbow locked.

-With the chest up, the stomach in, the spine straight, and the hands fully stretched, and conscious breathing, retain the position for 30 seconds. Over time, the duration can be gradually extended to 60 seconds.

-Return to normal.

-Relax for 10 to 15 seconds.

-Repeat the cycle 10 times.

-If nothing else to, do get into *Savasana* and follow other protocols as explained under *tadasana*.

Benefits: Strengthens overall body muscles, reduces heartburns, and flatulence. It also strengthens the leg ligaments. It helps in better digestion and works as prevention against sciatica.

Caution: Those with asthma or other breathing problems, ladies with menstruation pain or problems can sit with the back against a wall to ease the stress of stretched back and an erect spine.

## 5. Swastikasana (cross-legged)

-Sit as in *Dandasana*.

-Bend the knees.

-Bring the right foot under the left thigh and the left foot under the right thigh.

-This is the cross-leg position. Place the right wrist on the right knee and the left wrist on the left knee with palms open and facing up.

-Keep the neck and the spine in a relaxed position, but straight.

-Continue with a conscious slow breathing throughout.

-Retain the posture for 30 seconds. The duration can be gradually extended to 60 seconds and more.

-Relax for 10 seconds.

-Repeat 10 times.

Benefit: Relaxes tired legs, provides suppleness to hip joints, and strengthens the knee cartilage. It is also helpful in spiritual meditation.

## 6. Virasana

-Bend the knees backward.

-Bring the knees together.

-The sole of the feet to face up and separated from each other.

-The outer edge of the thigh to rest on the foot sole.

Note: For ease of comfort, a soft folded blanket can be placed under the buttocks, feet, and the knees.

-The torso to be pulled in. Back straightened up and the spine to be erect.

-The neck and the head in the normal position but firmly placed.

-Bring the palms closer to the respective knees. Place the palms on the knees and lock the elbow.

-With focused and normal breathing, retain this position for a minute.

-Over time, the duration can be increased up to 5 minutes.

-Relax for 10 to 15 seconds.

-Repeat the process 10 times.

-If nothing else, get into *savasana* to finish the day.

**Benefits:**

For those standing for long hours, this *asana* will be extremely useful. It relieves the pain in the calves, ankles, and heels. It also tones the hamstring muscles.

Caution: General caution in yoga is never to overdo. If you have any affliction and pain, avoid yoga until you have addressed the issue.

## 7. Padmasana

It is also called the 'Lotus' posture. It is the most preferred *asana* for meditation and *Sadhana*. This posture is widely adopted for spiritual awakening. Bhawan Budhha is popularly shown in this posture. It is said that He attained His enlightenment in this posture while meditating under a Peepal tree at Gaya (in Bihar, India).

**Procedure:**

-Sit on the firm surface with the back straight, spine erect, and legs stretched forward.

-Bend the right leg, hold the right foot with both hands, and place it on the left thigh with the sole facing up. The heel of the foot must be as close to the navel as possible.

-Bend the left leg, hold the foot with both hands and place it over the right thigh with the heel close to the navel and sole facing up.

-Bring the right palm on the right knee and the left palm on the left knee.

-Keep the knuckles on the respective knees, palms open and facing up, the tip of the index finger in contact with the tip of the thumb.

-This posture is also called *Gyan Mudra* (knowledge pose).

-Hold the neck and head normal, but firmly in place.

-Sit in this posture for 1 to 3 minutes with conscious breathing.

-If needed, relax in between, and repeat.

-A 15-minute *Padmasana* over time will prepare you for the advanced stage of concentration.

**Benefits:**

Optimises heart functioning and improves blood circulation. It helps control the mind and stimulates consciousness.

## 8. Sirsasana (headstand)

*Sirsa* in Sanskrit is head. It is the inversion of our normal posture. It implies standing on one's head. It is considered as one the most important yoga postures but with certain restrictions and caution.

First the caution part:

-Not to be practised by persons with backaches, cervical spondylosis, migraine, or headache.

-Not to be practised during menstruation.

-Never start a yoga routine with the headstand.

-In one session, do not do it more than once.

**Procedure:**

1. Accessory: Soft folded blanket on a firm surface for head support.

2. Sit in the virasana pose.

3. Bend forward with your fingers interlocked.

4. Place the palms on the blanket with arms separated and on the floor of the surface.

5. Raise the thighs and the waistline. Bring the skull in contact with the palms.

6. Straighten up the legs with heels up and toes pressing the floor.

7. Give a gentle push with the toes and bring forward the folded legs in contact with the stomach.

8. Balance the body with the support of the palms and the skull well placed in the palms.

9. Straighten up one leg. Balance the position.

10. Straighten up the other leg. Bring the feet together.

11. Straighten up the legs with stretch on calves and thigh.

12. Remain in this position for 3 to 5 minutes. During this period, keep breathing gently.

13. In a situation of discomfort, return to normal.

14. In the end, return to the normal posture gradually and gently. Sit straight for a minute. Breathe normally.

Beginners can start it with the support of a wall until they develop the art of balancing freely.

**Benefits:**

Good for stamina build-up.

Improves heart functioning.

Takes care of those suffering from insomnia.

Strengthens lungs.

Addresses the problem of halitosis.

## 9. SAVASANA (DEAD POSE)

*Savasana* is a posture that simulates a dead body. It is the easiest, yet most difficult of all the asanas. It is refreshing and highly rewarding.

### Technique:

-Lie flat on the back on a hard surface covered with a soft blanket or a cushioned mat.

-Keep the heels together, hands away from the body with palms facing up.

-Close the eyes.

-Leave the entire body loose and free of any stress.

-Take a deep slow breath in and breathe out gently without noise.

-Ensure that during breathing out, the air brushes past the upper jaw.

-Repeat the cycle initially for 5 minutes and increase gradually to 10, 15 and finally to 20 minutes.

-Throughout the process, nothing should move except the breath. All muscles to remain relaxed.

-Ensure that you are fully conscious of the entire breathing cycle and do not fall into sleep

or snore.

-In the end, fold the legs, turn on the right side, put the palms together under your head as a cushion and remain in this state for 3 to 5 minutes.

-Sit in an easy posture.

You should feel fully relaxed with no fatigue and no stress.

**Benefit:**

Soothes the nerves and calms the mind. With every inhale, you have the joy of receiving the life force in. Every exhale is an acknowledgement of gratitude.

# PRANAYAM (THE ART AND SCIENCE OF BREATHING)

*Pranayam* is usually considered as deep breathing. As a physical act that is what it is. But it goes far beyond it. *Pranayam* is the spine of *Astha Yoga*. It is the bridge that links the acquired benefits of the three earlier stages of *Yama*, *Niyam* and *Asana* with the next four *Pratyahar*, *Dharana*, *Dhyan* and *Samadhi*. The first three stages mould the pot. *Pranayam* bakes and strengthens the pot. The *Sadhaka* (practitioner) is now well-equipped to fill the pot with the nectar of wisdom and divine experiences that will accrue from *Dharana* (concentration), *Dhyan* (Meditation), and *Samadhi* (state of extended high-intensity concentration). It is therefore imperative to have an easy but correct understanding of the science and the art of *Pranayam*.

The word *Pranayam* is the synthesis of two words, *pran* and *ayam*. *Pran* literally means life force and *ayam* means extension and expansion. Thus,

*Pranayam* in simple terms is expanded and extended breathing. Expanded signifies that the lungs are full with a prolonged deep breath. Extended is the duration one can hold the breath in before slowly exhaling it out. It is only through expanded and extended breathing that optimum exchange of oxygen and carbon di- oxide can be possible. Strong torso and strong rib cage facilitate the expanded and extended breathing. Therefore necessary exercise and asana must be part of yoga routine in order to strengthen the torso muscles and rib cage.

*Pran* is not just the air we breathe. It is a symbol of vital cosmic energy that we extract, produce, retain, and use. It is believed that the entire cosmos is nothing but energy in various forms. *Pran* can be termed as a synonym of energy. By extension therefore, the entire universe is energy with. In all animate creatures *pran* is manifested with birth. It escapes with death. Realisation that life is nothing but existence of Pran(some call it soul) in the physical body and its escape is death will free one from fear of death. There are many quotes of wisdom related to life and death. Death is of the body not of the soul or the life force that simply escapes to enter another body. Saint Kabir says;

"Das dware ka pinjara,

Tame panchhi ek,

Awat ko acharaj nahi,

Jaye to acharaj hoi."

(Text meaning of the verse is that this body is like a cage with ten door, two eyes, two ears, two nostrils, one mouth, two organs of reproduction and discharge and one Brahmarandra, great hole in the crown of the head. No one is surprised when the soul or the life force enters the body and resides therein under the guard of the ten doors. Why should one be surprised or feel sad when it escapes? It establishes the fact that the death of the body is not the end of the soul or the life force. Life force or the soul is eternal. It simply changes its abode.)

Bhagwat Gita, the holy scripture says;

"Na jayate mriyate va kadachit,

Na ayam bhutwa bhavita va na bhuyah,

Ajo nityaha sashwat ayam purano,

Na hanyate hanyamane sharire."

Verse 20, chapter 2. Gita.

(Meaning of the verse: Referring to the nature of the soul Lord Krishna says; It is never born nor dies; nor its existence is dependent on any birth or death. It is eternal and continues to live even after the body is dead).

Death in reality is continuation of the journey to another form and phase of life. So why remorse?

Having briefly touched the eternal nature of Soul or life force let us revert back to the art and science of pranayam, the process whose conscious application can enable us to progress in our journey to self realisation. First, let us try to understand the science of *pranayam*. The human body has four prominent systems whose proper functioning is important for a healthy life. These are respiratory, circulatory, digestive and excretory. These are mutually interdependent. At the same these are distinct in their functioning and goals. The building blocks of these systems and their various components are the atoms and cells (like any other mass or matter). Atoms consist of a nucleus with neutrons and protons and electrons moving around in fixed orbits. An atom is confined in a space of the size of 100 millionth of a centimetre. The nucleus is confined in a space of the size of one hundred thousand times smaller to the size of the atom. Confined in these tiny tight spaces, the particles are always in a state of unease and motion. The electrons revolve at a speed of nearly 1,000 km (600 miles) an hour and the neutrons and protons revolve at a speed of 64,000 km (40,000 miles) an hour. These particles want to escape from the tight confinement. Alternatively, they may combine with other atoms to form more stable matter. There are two possible options. One, the product emerging from the two or more atoms is stable with totally different characteristics to the constituent atoms. The second possibility is that the particles escape and there is the disintegration of an atom. There is a third option too, impingement from a free particle. Impingement often results in a chain reaction. In the process huge amount of energy is either absorbed or released in the form of heat and electromagnetic waves. This is a continuous phenomenon at the cosmic level and the radioactive substances. Each of these activities is associated with exchange of energy in various forms and frequencies. Essentially the entire cosmos is filled with energy or its manifestation as mass and matter. These mass and matter appear and disappear. Matter and mass undergo the cycle of birth and death. Energy is eternal.

From the viewpoint of medical science the fundamental building block of the body is the cell. It has been identified that in an average human body there is estimated to be 37 trillion (37,000,000,000,000) cells, some 60 trillion (60,000,000,000,000) bacteria (mostly in the gut), and nearly 100 billion (100,000,000,000) neurons. Sustenance of these building blocks is through the right amount and regular supply of energy in the form of protein, nutrients, and carbohydrates. Lack of proteins and nutrients, or their occasional shortage can cause discomfort and disease. One of the primary purposes of *Pranayam* is to extract, generate, store, and distribute sufficient energy to each of the constituent particles and all the organs. Thus far we have been able to realise the energy equation for a healthy body and mind system. We shall now try to understand the nature of energy, what it is and what it does?

## What is energy?

Work done on a system or an object over a period of time is energy. In the process the system absorbs energy. On the contrary when a system is engaged in doing a work it delivers energy. This is basic form of energy exchange which we often see in our routine activities. Thus any movement or disturbed state of matter and mind, local or distant in the universe, is the cause of either creating energy or consuming energy. We shall see briefly is the incomprehensible magnitude of mass and energy exchange in the cosmos. Cosmos is filled with clusters of galaxies and stars. According to the astronomers at NASA, one of such cluster is known as J0454.1-0300 and has a mass around 180 trillion (180, 000,000,000,000) times the mass of the Sun. The mass of Sun itself is estimated at 1,989,000,000,000,000,000,000,000,000tons (approximately two trillion trillion tons). The reason for writing the numerals in the expanded form is to give the reader a sense of the large dimensions and huge mass we are going to talk about in context to the universal mass and energy. About 1,300,000 Earths can fit inside the Sun. The mass of the Sun is 333,000 times the mass of Earth. The Sun contributes to almost 99.8 per cent of the total mass of the Solar System. It may be the biggest entity in the Solar System and yet, it is average compared to other stars. Further, there are galaxies with billions of stars. Search continues and every day there are new additions. In fact study of the cosmos is an endless process. The issue like dark matter is still a mystery. So is time and life. Scientists, individually and collectively, are busy to find the origin and nature of cosmic **energy, time, and life**. No acceptable data or theory has been obtained in regard to time and life. The universal and eternal nature of energy however has been well accepted and established. Hindu Sages learnt the art of filtering the right quality and quantity of cosmic energy in their own body mind system. They also knew the art of using these energies for welfare of humanity. They realised that Time, Life and Energy are eternal.

The world of science is still on the periphery of the Time and Life concept. Following quotes from some of the famous scientific minds is a testimony to their ultimate faith in God and His mind.

**'If final answers (are) to be achieved, we will have to go beyond science.'**

David Shiang in his book, *God Does Not Play Dice*.

**'The ultimate triumph of human reason is to know the mind of God.'**

Stephen Hawking.

**'There are times when one feels liberated from one's limits and human imperfections. Life and death fuse together and there is neither evolution nor destination, there is only Being.'**

Albert Einstein, a scientist and philosopher of great eminence.

The philosophy and principles of spiritual world of Hinduism has evolved through self experience, revelation and astronomical calculation. As per our scriptures time, energy and life are eternal and limitless. But these are not endless. More about it may be at a later stage. Currently our focus will be on understanding yoga as a tool and a process to know the self. The above introduction regarding energy as a universal concept will help our understanding of *pran* or energy in life context.

There are three ways that energy is generated or received in the body system.

Firstly, the food we eat and water and other fluids we drink. These, when properly digested result in energy, muscles, fat, and waste. On an average the conversion ratio to mass has been found as below:

Energy – 10 per cent of the total intake.

Muscles and fat 30 to 40 per cent of the intake.

Waste – 50 to 60 per cent of the intake.

Even with the high nutrient value the ratio remains in the indicated range. Some energy booster foods or drinks can stimulate the system to meet immediate emergency needs or create excitement of transitory nature.

Second; Oxygenated Energy.

This involves the natural and basic function of *Pranayam*; breathing. We can also classify it as the science of breathing. All living organisms breathe and respirate. In breathing there is an exchange of oxygen that is absorbed in the blood and carbon dioxide, a product of toxic accumulation in the body, is extracted out. The blood, through the vast network of a tubular pipe-like structure called arteries and veins, provides oxygen and glucose to the trillions of cells. Oxidisation helps in elimination of waste, while glucose, a respiratory product, supplied with the oxygen provides the energy for healthy performance of the cells. This exchange of oxygen and carbon dioxide in the bloodstream occurs through the lungs.

Functioning of the lungs, the breathing process, and the fluid carrier network detail will help in understanding the nuances of *Pranayam*.

**Lungs in the Human Body**

All humans have a pair of lungs. One is situated on the left side and is relatively smaller in size and the other is situated on the right side. The left lung has two lobes, and the right lung has three lobes. The lobes contain the spongy air-filled sacs called alveoli. The windpipe situated in the throat is approximately six centimetres long with a diameter of roughly two centimetres. This windpipe further divides into two primary bronchi, one leading to the left lung and the other to the right. These further divide into tiny bronchioles finally connecting to the alveoli, the tiny air sacs like the bunch of grapes. The cluster of sacs is covered with a thin expandable membrane called pleura which inflates and deflates like a balloon. When air is sucked into the lungs, oxygen from the air is absorbed into the blood. In exchange, carbon dioxide and the waste product of metabolism, is exhaled. The oxygenated blood is then supplied to the billions of body cells that use it to generate the much-needed energy in the body system.

Some 300 million sacs line each lung. If opened and spread out these will measure approximately 80 square metres, almost 50 times the area of human skin. The average lung capacity in a grown-up person is six litres (6,000 cc). In involuntary breathing, the average quantum of the air we breathe in is between 300 to 500 cc. The blood carriers, arteries, and veins consist of some six billion networks totalling 10,000 kms in length. The heart pumps the blood through the body at a rate of seventy times per minute. It is therefore extremely critical that these components are kept in as perfect a condition as possible for a healthy body and mind upkeep.

Breathing is natural. Involuntary breathing starts with life and goes out with life. For the initial years of life covering childhood to youth, involuntary breathing is ably supported by physical activities. These ensure optimum use of the lungs. The energy acquired through oxygenation of the blood is sufficient to meet the overall requirement of the gross and subtle bodies. As years pass by, health issues manifest in one form or the other. These issues and resultant afflictions, in addition to other reasons, can be directly associated with the short supply or the underutilisation of energy. Invariably, it has been observed that the problem begins with the below par functioning of the lungs. The first impact of any minor or major disease is reflected in the depth and cycle of breathing. A suffering person is advised dietary change or the use of medicine as immediate relief. During this period of recovery there is hardly any attention paid to the proper functioning of lungs. The lung efficiency deteriorates due to lack of utilisation. The supplements become a routine intake and health gets a hit. In the process, we commit the following unintended mistakes:

-The poor depth and quality of breathing resulting in the underutilisation of lung capacity. This renders unused sacs or alveoli dormant and over time less and less effective, leading to eventual dysfunction.

-Poor retention, thus less time to absorb oxygen and discharge carbon dioxide.

-Both above lead to poor energy conversion, thereby causing digestive and circulatory problems.

-Poor or inefficient performance of lungs will lead to other health-related complications beginning with short breathing to fatigue, lack of stamina, loss of sleep, reduced concentration, and poor ability to perform.

## ART OF CONSCIOUS BREATHING – PRANAYAM.

'Breath is the key to ultimate emancipation.'

Swetmarma

(15th-century saint)

We shall now try to understand the art of correct and conscious breathing. Involuntary breathing is an auto mechanism. It just suffices to provide the survivable energy to the body and mind. It is incapable of providing the robustness and ability to fight the health hazards at the time of need. It also underutilises the lungs leading to system weakness and ultimate singular and complex failures. The quality of life undergoes undesirable and forced compromises. All these can be overcome with self-commitment and practice with perseverance.

Through proper understanding and practice of *Pranayam*, one can enhance the lung capacity by extended and expanded breathing. *Pranayam* is more than just extended and expanded breathing. It keeps the vital nervous system clean and healthy. It enables an enhanced level of concentration. It is a self-regulated auto-mechanism to extract cosmic energy within the body. Finally, it prepares the practitioner to achieve the ultimate goal. We shall address these in the subsequent chapters on *Dharna*, *Dhyan*, and *Samadhi*. Our present focus will be on breathing and *Pranyam*.

A normal breathing cycle consists of inhalation, retention, exhalation, and retention. This process makes a cycle. In an average person, under normal conditions, the breathing cycle is 18 to 20 in a minute. It is involuntary breathing. The duration, depth, and quality of breathing are low by all counts. In such breathing only upper part of the lung is utilised. Wheras the concentration of alveoli, the grape like bunch, is located at the lower end of the lung. As a result blood from the heart has less time and surface area to interact and exchange the much-needed oxygen and transfer out carbon dioxide. The body cells obtain less oxygen and proportionately less energy is available to the system. The other disadvantage is the possible retention of toxins in the system. Less of oxygen and more of carbon-di-oxide makes the body a vulnerable breeding field for ailment.

Extended and expanded voluntary breathing with the right posture is the first step to learning *Pranayam*. As one advances over time, valuable and rewarding features of *Pranayam* will be experienced. It aids in realisation and creation of *pran*, the life force. It also works as a catalyst to create a fusion of water and fire. This becomes possible when the practitioner has reached an advanced state of pranayam. We shall further touch this in the chapter on meditation.

There are nearly 200 (two hundred) ways to breathe. Each has its own specific cause and effect. The basic objective remains the optimum utilisation of the lungs and energy acquisition, cleansing of the tubular energy carriers and keeping these healthy.

'We must generate sufficient energy to realise our full potential. Only cosmic energy can take us there.'
B.K.S. Iyengar

## Basic tenets of Yoga

1. Yoga by itself is not therapeutic or curative in nature. It is to predominantly provide a healthy, firm, flexible, and robust body, a disciplined mind, and a sharp intellect. Its constant practise will also lead to:

a. Healthy loss of appetite.

b. An increased loss of interest in the material world of possessions.

2. Yoga, under guidance, can assist in faster recovery and rehabilitation, post any major surgical procedure. In essence, yoga is neither advisable nor possible to be practised by a sick or unhealthy person. Even during practice, if there is a feeling of discomfort or unbearable pain, one should pause and ascertain whether to continue or not.

3. Commitment with the self to practice yoga on a regular basis unless sick or unwell. Laziness is the worst enemy of yoga.

4. Yoga to be practised alone or under a Guru but never in a mass. Yoga demands a high level of concentration and conscious involvement.

5. Prefer an open space and a clean environment.

6. Yoga should preferably be done on an empty stomach and empty bladder. If there is time constraint it can be done half an hour after a light meal or two hours after a heavy meal.

## Preparation for Pranayam

Accessories needed:

A mat with moderate soft cushioning or a blanket.

A hard surface (floor or a bed with wooden top).

A small wet towel.

A glass of water.

Bare feet.

Dress basic and not tight fit, something which will not restrict movement.

## Postures

Following four postures are common:

# 1. Padmasana

Technique:

Spread the mat or the blanket on the floor or the surface of choice.

Sit with the back straight and legs stretched in front.

Bend the right leg, hold the right foot with both hands and place it on the left thigh. The right foot heel to be as close to the navel as possible.

Next, bend the left leg, hold the left foot with both the hands and place it on the right thigh with the heel near the navel.

Soles of the feet to face up

Place the back of the right palm on the right knee and the back of the left palm on the left knee with tip of the thumbs touching the tip of the respective index fingers. Leave the arms loose and palms facing up.

Once again focus on your back. Ensure that the spine, from the base to the neck remains firm and straight throughout.

Set to start

For ease refer the related plate.

# 2. Siddhasana

Similar preparations as under *Padmasana*

Technique:

Sit on the hard surface with the back straight and legs stretched in front.

Bend the left leg at the knee. Bring the left foot to rest under the right thigh with the sole of the left foot facing up.

Bend the right leg at the knee and place the right foot in between the calf and thigh of the left leg with the soles facing up.

Bring the back of the palms to rest on the respective knees as in *Padmasana* with tips of the thumb and index finger touching each other and the palms facing up. Arms to remain loose, spine shall remain straight and firm from base to the neck.

You are ready to start.

For correct posturing refer the relevant plate.

## 3. Sukhasana

All pre-posturing preparations shall be the same as under *Padmasana*.

Technique:

Sit with the back straight on the hard surface.

Stretch the legs in front.

Bend the right leg at the knee. Hold the foot with the two hands and bring it under the left leg to rest in between the calf and the thigh. Sole should face up.

Bend the left leg and using the two hands bring the left foot under right leg to rest between the calf and the thigh. Sole should face up.

Palms and arm position as in *Padmasana*.

Once again, ensure that the spine is firm and straight from the base to the neck.

You are set to start.

For correct posturing refer the relevant plate.

## 4. Virasana

All pre-posture preparations are similar to the one under *Padmasana*.

Technique:

Bend back both the legs at the knee.

Bring the knees together.

Separate the feet.

Rest the sides of the hips on the soles of the feet.

Sit with the spine firm and straight.

You are ready to start.

For correct posturing refer the relevant plate.

Note: Those who are elderly or infirm, may opt for other convenient postures in consultation with the right *Guru* (teacher).

It has been mentioned earlier that there are two hundred ways to breathe. Each has a separate cause and effect. It will be better that we limit ourselves to some select few of these which can be practised by the generality of the people without the severity of the procedure and yet derive optimum benefit. With this in consideration, I have selected the following few and have described the technique and their benefits. These are:

1. *Ujjayi Pranayam*

2. *Surya Bhedan Pranayam*

3. *Nadi Shodhan Pranayam*

4. *Anulom Pranayam*

5. *Vilom Pranayam*

6. Bhramari Pranayam

7. *Savasana*

Before we get into the step-by-step technique of accomplishing these *pranayam* types, it will be useful to understand the meaning and methods of some common terminologies that will often be used in the process of practice.

*Mula Bandha*: *Mula* in Sanskrit means 'root.' *Bandh* is 'dam.' Damming of the root is *Mula Bandha*.

In actual practise, it means, a posture where the part between the anus and the navel is contracted and lifted.

*Jal Bandha*: *Jal* is 'net' and *bandha* is 'dam.' Damming of the net is *jal bandha*. In actual practice, it involves lowering of the neck from the nape, lift the torso, rest the chin on the collar bone. That is *Jal Bandha*.

Retention: It involves the stoppage of breath after inhalation and also after exhalation. Accordingly, we call retention after inhalation and retention after exhalation. The retention part shall be applied only after the practitioner has acquired enough control over the breathing techniques. Retention after exhalation should be tried only under supervision or when the practitioner has self-acquired competence and confidence.

Time now to proceed with the details of the techniques:

## UJJAYI PRANAYAM

1. Adopt one of the four positions explained earlier that is, *Padmasana*, *Siddhasana*, *Sukhasana*, and *Virasana*. For any disability reason, if none of these postures are possible, then adopt any convenient and comfortable posture you can maintain for the duration of the practice.

2. Stretch the arms out and place the backside of the right palm on the right knee and the left palm in the same fashion on the left knee.

3. Close the eyes. No stress. Concentrate on the breathing sequence.

4. Exhale completely, pull up the torso and bring the chin on the collar bone (*Jal Bandha*).

5. Inhale slow and prolonged. Fill the lungs to the brim. Pull the stomach area in towards the spine. Feel the inhale brushing the inner passage of the sinus area.

6. Retain the breath for a few seconds without causing discomfort.

7. Exhale slowly and completely. Feel the out-breath brushing the outer passage of the sinus area. As you advance, the out-breath will brush the surface of the upper jaw. Give a little break without altering the posture.

NOTE: Throughout processes 1 to 7, nothing will move except the breath, not even the eyelids or the iris.

1 to 7 completes one cycle of the *Ujjayi Pranayam*.

8. Repeat 1 to 7 for the duration you can comfortably and **consciously** do. Gradually increase it by a cycle each day. Share experiences and / or problems with a guru (teacher). 25 cycles a day should be the aim for real benefit and joy. Should there be time constraints, divide it into two sittings. The more you do, the more you gain.

If no other activity, go into *Savasana*.

Benefits of *Ujjayi Prāṇayam*:

Aerates the lungs, removes phlegm, enhances endurance, and tones up the entire system.

It can be practised by all age groups. The only restriction is one's own ability. Those with severe high blood pressure can adopt a reclining posture.

## SURYABHEDI PRANAYAM

**In this pranayam, breath is inhaled from the right nostril and exhaled from the left in the manner described below.**

1. Adopt the posture from 1 to 4 as in *Ujjayi Pranayam*.

2. Use the right-hand fingers in the manner as stated below to control the breathing process:

    -Thumb on the root of the right nostril

    -The little finger on the root of the left nostril

    -Remaining three fingers bent towards the palm

3. Close the left nostril completely using the little finger. If required, support of the ring finger can be obtained.

4. Apply modest thumb pressure on the fatty tissue of the right nostril to align it parallel to the lower edge of the cartilage of the spectrum.

5. Inhale slowly and deeply from the right nostril. Fill the lungs to the full extent as possible. Hold the breath for 3 to 6 seconds.

6. Using the thumb to close the right nostril completely. Allow partial opening of the left nostril and breathe out slowly and smoothly.

7. Action 1 to 6 makes one cycle. Repeat the cycle 8 to 10 times. Increase it by one cycle a day till you can comfortably do 25 cycles in one sitting.

8. Relax for 10 seconds. If no additional yoga activity, go into *savasana* (dead pose) and follow the protocol as described under the essential protocol of *Pranayam*.

## BENEFITS:

It cleanses the sinuses, invigorates the lungs, and improves digestion.

It is also good for people with low blood pressure. Persons with high blood pressure may avoid it.

## NADI SODHAN PRANAYAM.

*Nadi* in the Sanskrit language means the tubular organ in the body that carries the food, fluid, and energy to the entire system.

*Sodhan* is cleaning.

*Nadi Sodhan Pranayam*, therefore, is a mechanism to keep the arteries and veins not only healthy, but also clean to facilitate the uninterrupted supply of nourishment and energy to each cell and organ of the body.

### Technique:

1. Step 1 to 4 as in *Surya Bhedan Pranayam*.

2. Inhale slowly and deeply with the right nostril.

3. Close the right nostril completely. Exhale slowly from the left nostril.

4. Keep the right nostril closed and inhale slow and deep with the left nostril. Close the left nostril completely and exhale from the right nostril. Remember, unless advised, inhale and exhale shall never be forced or abrupt action.

5. Action 1 to 4 makes one cycle. Repeat ten times. Increase by a cycle a day.

6. If no other yoga action, go into *Savasana* (dead pose) and follow the protocol.

**Benefits:**

Improves the supply of oxygen to the blood and brings freshness, vigour, and calm.

# ANULOM PRANAYAM.

*Anu* is 'with,' *lome* in Sanskrit is 'hair' (here it refers to the hair in the nostrils). 'With the hair' implies natural breathing. This is one *Pranayam* which has the combined benefits of *Ujjayi*, *Nadi Sodhan*, and *Surya Bhedan*.

Technique:

1 Adopt the action 1 to 4 as in *Ujjayi Pranayam*.

2. Exhale completely.

3. Inhale with both the nostrils, slow and deep till the lungs are full.

4. Pull the stomach in and bring *Mul Bandha* into action.

5. Position the right-hand fingers on the nostrils as in *Surya Bhedan*.

6. Close the left nostril completely. Exhale slowly with the right nostril. Relax the *Mul Bandh*.

7. Inhale with both the nostrils as in 3 above. Pull the stomach in. Bring the right-hand fingers in action. Activate *Mul Bandha*.

8. Close the right nostril. Exhale from the left nostril. Relax *Mul Bandha*.

9. 3 to 8 above complete one cycle. Start with 8 to 10 cycles, increase it by one cycle each successive day till you can do 25 cycles in one sitting. You can add further as you advance, and time permits.

10. If no other action, get into *Savasana* and follow the protocol.

## NOTE OF CAUTION:

In this *Pranayam*, exhalation will be longer than inhalation (a non-rhythmic cycle). This should be practised only by those who have better control of breathing or do it under guidance.

**Not recommended for persons suffering from disorders of the heart or the nervous system.**

# VILOME PRANAYAM.

*Vilom* in Sanskrit is 'opposite' or 'not with the trend.' It can also be called break breathing.

This *Pranayam* is done in two stages:

First stage:

Adopt the postures 1 to 4 as in *Ujjayi Pranayam*.

Exhale completely. Inhale with a break, that means, inhale for a second or two, pause for a second or two, inhale again in the same fashion with a pause. Continue till the lungs are filled to the brim. Activate *Mul Bandha*. Exhale slowly with *Mul Bandha* relaxed.

Second Stage:

Rest for a minute or two. Get into the preparatory posture. Inhale normally in one continuous slow rhythm with *mool bandha* in action. Pause briefly, relax *mool bandha*, exhale with a break, that is controlled short exhale for a second or two, pause for a second or two. Continue the process until total exhalation.

The two stages together make a cycle.

Do it 8 to 10 times. If no other activity, get into *Savasana* and follow the protocol.

**Benefit:**

Stage 1 is helpful to those with low blood pressure and stage two will be beneficial to those with high blood pressure.

# BHRAMARI PRANAYAM

*Bhramari* resonates the sound of a bee. The practitioner should generate a similar sound while practising this *Pranayam*. It is an easy process.

**Technique:**

1. Follow 1 to 4 as in *Ujjayi Pranayam*.

2. Fold the two hands from the elbow. Bring them up to your face. Block the right ear with the right thumb and the left ear with the left thumb.

3. Softly place the index finger together with the middle finger of the right hand on to the right eye. Likewise, do the same on the left eye with the fingers of the left hand.

4. Place the ring finger of the right hand on the outer soft tissue of the right nostril. Do likewise on the left nostril with the ring finger of the left hand.

5. Exhale completely. Do *Jal Bandha*. Inhale with both the nostrils to fill the lungs to the brim.

Activate *mool bandha*. Hold the breath for 3 to 6 seconds.

6. Exhale slowly with a humming sound by pressing the walls of the nostrils.

7. 5 and 6 above make a cycle. Try and do 8 to 10 cycles in one sitting. It can be increased gradually.

**Benefits:**

Stimulates sleep. Good for those suffering from insomnia.

## PROTOCOL OF PRANAYAM

The following forms the common principle and protocol of *Pranayam*:

1. *Pranayam* should be done on an empty stomach and an empty bladder.

2. It should be done with a clean body (preferably after a bath), in a clean place, and open-air (preferably).

3. The sitting base should be firm. In all the postures, the back must remain straight and firm. One way to ascertain this is to remain conscious of your posture and the back.

4. Eyes to remain closed throughout, vision drawn inward, and sight fixed on the tip of the nose.

5. No feeling of discomforting stress on any organ like eyes or the face.

6. All *pranayams* begins with exhaling and ends with inhaling. Breathing should always be slow, deep, and smooth unless desired otherwise.

7. Throughout, remain conscious of the breathing, its quality, and passage.

8. The last act shall always be *Savasana* (dead pose) and the first thing after *Savasana* shall be a glass of

water or juice. Give a gap of 15 minutes before taking a meal or any exercise.

9. Remember the 3 Ps: Practice, Perseverance and Patience.

10. Laziness is yoga's worst enemy. Overcome it.

## Important Note:

For the optimum benefit of *Pranayam*, it should be done on a regular basis at least once in a day of 30 to 45 minutes duration. The frequency and duration can be increased gradually to derive extra benefit and bliss.

Should there be a feeling of discomfort or an unnatural pain, stop *Pranayam* and consult the teacher. In a majority of the cases, a conscious practitioner develops an auto-correction mechanism.

With the knowledge and practice of *Yama*, *Niyam*, *Asanas*, and *Pranayam* the practitioner is now set to take the journey further to:

*Pratyahar*

*Dharana*

*Dhyan*

*Samadhi*

These are subtle in nature. The practise of these will reveal the true self. We shall see how (?) as we progress. Till then keep doing what you have learnt and enjoy the bliss and blessings of yoga.

# PRATYAHAR.

The first four stages of *Patanjali Astha Yoga* help in:
- Nurturing self-discipline.
- Adoption and application of life values.
- Provide healthy, robust, and firm body.
- Learning science and art of breathing -energy creation, distribution and storage.

*Pratyahar* is the fifth stage of *Patanjali Astha Yoga*. At this stage the practitioner (*sadhaka*) gradually unveils the mind sheath (*manomaya kosh*). Having addressed the need for the gross and physiological bodies (sheaths), the practitioner enters the arena of the mind. The mind is the veil covering intelligence, intellect, and consciousness. These are the centres to recognise sense perceptions and initiate action. Senses of perception create desire. Organs of action are applied to fulfil the desires. To gain control over desire is the aim of *pratyahar*. The intent is not forced denial of desires. It is the conscious rationalisation of desire. Need and greed are two determining factors of desire to possess, own and hold on to possessions. Persistent yoga results into an increasing loss of interest in material possessions.

Practiced over time greed dilutes, contentment becomes part of nature.

The self (soul) is considered to be under the veil of five sheaths (*koshas*). These are;

1. *Annamaya Kosh*, the gross body.

2. *Pranmaya Kosh*, the physiological body.

3. *Manomaya Kosh*, the perception sheath.

4. *Gyanmaya Kosh*, the knowledge sheath.

5. *Anandmaya Kosh*, the blissful sheath.

These sheaths are intricately interwoven. The first three stages of *Astha Yoga*: *yama*, *niyam*, and *asana* are mainly related to *annamaya kosh*. The fourth stage of *Astha Yoga*, *pranayam* is addresses the *pranmaya kosh*. The practitioner now has the essential tools in his armoury to address the third layer, the *manomaya kosh*. The organs of sense perception, if left untamed, are wild in nature. Whatever these can survey through vision, sound, taste, and touch cause strong desire to possess. Some of these possessions can be justified. These are need-based and are essential for existence. There are desires that are greed stimulated that primarily serve and satisfy the ego. Desires that are greed stimulated and those that enhance ego should be tamed and controlled.

When a sense perceives it activates the mind. The mind transmits it to the intelligence. Intelligence relates with the intellect. Intellect transmits it to consciousness. It is the conscious part of the mind that generates the decision and creates action impulse. The reverse flow is initiated. Either there is a command to act or deny the action. All these sequences are too fast in time reckoning and appear instantaneous. The decision based on conscious rationale will prevail. The decision based on conscious rationale is *pratyahar*.

'*Svavisaya asamprayoge cittasya svarupanukarah iva indriyanam pratyaharah.*'

Patanjali, sutra 54.

*Sva*: means: self, personal.

*Visaya*: means: material, object.

*Asamprayoge*: means: not in contact, not with the senses.

*Chittasya*: means: consciousness.

*Svarup*: means: form identification, shape.

*Anukarah*: means: desire, to copy.

*Iva*: means: if.

*Indriyanam*: means: senses.

*Pratyahar*: means: a pull in the opposite direction.

The translation of the *sutra* is;

Withdrawing the senses and consciousness away from the contact with the outside object and making an effort to look inward in identity with the self is *pratyahar*.

# DHARANA (CONCENTRATION)

To remain focused on an outside object, a picture, a sign, or even just a dot for a considerable period of time, is called Dharana, to hold on to. The nearest English synonym of Dharana is 'concentration.'

'Desa bandhah chittasya dharana.'

Patanjali, Sutra III-1

Desh: means: an object, a spot, a mark.

Bandhah: means: to bind, to become one with.

Chittasya: means: of mind, consciousness.

Dharana: means: concentration.

The meaning of the sutra is;

When the mind and the consciousness become one with an object, a spot, or a mark, it is said to be in a state of Dharana (concentration).

Dharana is the sixth stage of Astha Yoga. The practitioner is now like a baked pot with controlled desires, ready to receive the nectar from the yogic practices of Dharana, Dhyan and Samadhi. He stands at a point from where the road forks into two directions. One leads to the material world. The other leads to the spiritual world. The first one will be the world to provide all the sensual pleasures and joy with luxury, glory, and comfort. The practitioner is well equipped and capable to succeed and enjoy the material world with enhanced vigour, equanimity and poise.

The road to the spiritual world will be different. The journey becomes more arduous, solitary, and inward-looking. The nature of joy will be blissful and divine. The mystery of life and time will be resolved. The soul will feel the freedom from the physical bondage.

A clear understanding of concentration will be of significant help in our onward journey. After all extension of concentration in intensity and duration is Dhyan (meditation) and Samadhi.

In the initial stage the duration and intensity of concentration will be low. With regular practice there will be a gradual improvement in both parameters. To begin with concentration can be done with eyes open and on an outside object. The object should not be moving when the time duration is intended to be long. Short duration focus can be done on a moving object with eyes open

The position and posture of the practitioner can be situational and of his/her choice. Once a posture has been chosen the practitioner shall firmly maintain that posture throughout. With regular practice the act will become easy. Over time, if practised regularly, it will be a part of nature. The duration gets longer and the object gets closer. The practitioner is now set to get into an advanced state of concentration. To enable this to happen, the following is recommended:

-For longer duration, a sitting posture should be adapted. It can be one of the four as suggested under pranayam or any other suited to the practitioner.

-The posture shall always be straight and firm.

-The preferred time shall be the morning or evening hours.

-Solitude is the keyword.

-Eyes to remain closed throughout. As stated in the preceding paragraph act of short duration focus can be done with eyes open and object in motion. It is only to enhance the ability to focus or concentrate over a long duration and on a non moving object.

-Neck firmly placed on the shoulders. Alternatively, the practitioner should find it convenient to bend the neck and place the chin on the uplifted collar bone. It provides better stability.

-Choose the point or place on the body to concentrate on. Recommended spots are: the tip of the nose, the centre of the eyebrows, and the navel.

-Start with conscious control of breath. Gradually shift the consciousness to the object. Mind, by nature, will flitter. Let it go. Bring it back. This ping pong game will decide the end game. Once you succeed in merging this ping pong ball with the object a state of indescribable feeling will be generated within. You will be moving from pleasure to joy to a state of bliss. You will have developed the art of dharna or concentration as part of your nature.

-How to come out of the state of Dharana? It should not be done in a hurry. Exit process should be gradual. Shift your focus from the object to breathing. Feel a slow and steady breathing cycle. Do it for a minute or two. Gradually open the eyes. Sip some liquid, preferably water.

**Benefit: Ability to focus in itself is a benefit; add to it enhanced memory and productivity. It gives poise, peace, and tranquillity. It prepares the practitioner for an easy entry into the next phase, that is, of meditation.**

# DHYAN (MEDITATION)

In my brief to the book, there is a mention of the word, 'meditation' as some kind of trademark for yoga. Meditation is the most critical and demanding stage of yoga. Its proper understanding therefore, becomes important to the practitioner and the teacher alike. If practised without the strengthening of all the body faculties, be it physical, physiological, pranic (energy) or intellectual, the risk can be hazardous. Only those who have practised all the six preceding stages with dedication should attempt meditation.

Meditation literally is the extension of concentration with a difference. Meditation is preferably done in a sitting posture over a long period of time. The chosen posture can be any of the ones described under pranayam. Invariably, concentration is a deep focus on an object, moving or still, for a short duration, where the eyes remain open. We often hear in study classes, instructions such as, "concentrate on your studies" or on a football pitch, we hear the coach say, "keep your eyes on the ball." These are short duration intense focus on an object or an act.

With regard to meditation, the object is always stationary and is located either on or within the body. Sage Vyas described certain suitable parts, to begin with. These are the centre of the eyebrows, the tip of the nose or the root of the tongue. The third and most important difference is the state of the eyes. The eyes shall remain closed and without movement. Even the pupil shall not move.

Sitting base: The practitioner will sit on a firm base. If needed, a soft blanket or folded sheet can be used. Once a chosen posture has been adopted, it will not alter for the duration of the meditation. If the time duration is more than two hours, one change can be permitted. Throughout the meditation, the posture shall remain firm and the spine straight. No movement of the body and no flittering of the mind are the mantras of meditation.

Time Duration: One can start with 30 minutes and gradually extend up to four hours.

"Tatra pratyaya ekatanata dhyanam."

Patanjali

Tatra: means there.

Pratyaya: means firm conviction.

Ekatanata: means uninterrupted, continuous.

Dhyanam: means concentration.

The meaning of the Sutra is:

A firm and unbroken flow of concentration is Dhyan (meditation).

The toughest task in meditation is the cessation of thoughts.

"Chittavritti nirodhah" (Cessation of movement of mind)

The mind has a flitting nature. It is the nerve centre of all activities. It receives and records information collected through the senses. It analyses and initiates action. It has a memory to retain identity and events. It has the ability to retrieve and reflect. It is the cause of all the Gunas (Sato, Rajo and Tamo). From an entity with acts so widely spread we want total detachment.

"Dhyanam Nirvisayam Manah"

"Ragopahtirdhyanam"

Samkhya Sutra

Dhyan demands a total detachment from all thoughts and impressions. One should focus only on the object so chosen, with the full awareness and knowledge of the fact that complete surrender to the creator and His Supreme nature is the way forward.

"Nasti Dhyanam Bina Gyanam"

Dhyan (meditation) is not possible without (proper) knowledge.

Pure and Sattwik Dhyan has been defined in Bhagwat Gita as:

"Dhritya yaya dharayate manah pranindriyakriyah,

Yogenavyabicharniya dhritih sa Parth sattwaki."

Chapter 18, verse 33.

Dhriti: means firmness.

Yaya: means by which.

Dharayate: means control, to hold.

Manah: refers to the mind.

Pran: means air (that we breathe).

Indriya: means senses (five of action and five of perception).

Avyabicharniya: means unwavering, firm.

Sa: means that.

Parth: refers to Arjun.

Sattviki: means pure, unblemished, good for all

Our existence is through a realisation of senses and the breath that gives life. In the above verse, the good Lord addresses Arjun and conveys the meaning and fruit of true meditation. He says, "The pure form (sattvik) of meditation is the firm control of the functions of the mind and senses including the vital air one breathes in." The emphasis is on the word firm, firm control on all senses, mind and life force, the breath.

The control of functions of the mind and senses is a state of total stillness. When the mind is controlled, the senses cease their functions and remain peaceful. It is the beginning of the realisation of a divine vision. The practitioner can see the colour and form of the mind and all the senses. When stillness is achieved, one can see the rays of the mind coming into contact with the indriyas, the senses. When the mind becomes one with the indriyas, it creates a special throb or ripple whenever it accepts the sense impressions. When the mind and the intellect are steady, extraordinary actions and reactions emerge. These can only be felt, but cannot be expressed. In his book, *Science of Soul*, Swami Yogeswaranand Saraswati describes this state of mind and intellect as below:

"These things cannot be described adequately in words. Only by the matured vision of meditation are they seen in the true form. With eyes closed one can see objects like stars or globules of light of different colours '' radiating from the centre of the eye brows. These are pure lights with no heat value. All senses are like circular points of lights. These can be distinctly seen in the state of deep meditation and mind activating the particular sense."

In the chapter on concentration we described a step-wise method to develop the art of concentration. We started with an object of focus outside the body. The duration of the focus will initially be short, but with consistent effort, the duration gets longer. With repeated efforts, it becomes part of nature. It opens the door to understanding the matter of mind and spirit. In conclusion, some basic rules and protocols were stated to enable prolonged concentration with closed eyes and a firm posture. In meditation, the period will get longer with the object of focus getting more subtle.

We often come across the words 'subtle body' and 'aura.' What is a subtle body? What is aura? The physical body is also called the gross body. It has a shape, a colour and a mass. The gross body is surrounded by energy layers. These energy layers generate an electromagnetic field that engulfs the gross body. When the intensity of the field is high, it becomes visible to the naked eyes and that is called aura. Some even call it subtle, astral or spiritual body. In shape, it is exactly the shape and form of the gross body. Where does this energy come from?

We have seven main energy centres within the body. These energy centres are called 'Chakras' (wheel). These are located along the spine, starting from coccyx up to the crown of the head. The details of the names and locations are;

1 Muladhara (root) chakra perineum, between the anus and genitals.

2. Swadhisthan (sacral) chakra lower stomach, below the belly button.

3. Manipura, Solar plexus chakra, located in the peritoneal cavity.

4. Anahata (heart) chakra in the chest area, close to the heart.

5. Vishudhi (purity) chakra in the throat area.

6. Ajna (knowledge) chakra in between the eyebrows, centre of the forehead.

7. Sahasrara (thousand petals) chakra crown of the head.

These chakras lie dormant in the normal body-mind state. These can be awakened with deep and prolonged meditation. Each awakened chakra reveals long lost memories and the truths of life. It opens the door to emancipation. It generates and preserves energy. The awakening of each chakra is related to the spiritual hierarchy of the practitioner in the following ascending order:

| | |
|---|---|
| Root Chakra | Shrutarishi |
| Swadhisthan chakra | Kandarishi |
| Manipura chakra | Paramarishi |
| Anahata chakra | Maharishi |
| Vishudhi chakra | Rajarshi |
| Ajna chakra | Devarshi |
| Sahasrara chakra | Brahmarshi |

To go into the merits, the power and potentials of these spiritual masters will be a lengthy task. We shall limit ourselves to the fact that, during the process of awakening, the practitioner directs energy from down to the top. This implies freeing himself from the earthly bondage of life. Understanding the potential of the mind and spirit gets clearer. At any stage, the trend can be reversed. The flow of energy reverses from top to down and the earthly bondage increases. The awakening of the first three chakras can be a great fulfiller of earthly gains and glory. The last four chakras lead to emancipation and freedom of the soul.

In conclusion, here are some practical tips related to meditation:

1. Anyone who has not acquired proficiency in the preceding stages of astha yoga should not attempt meditation. Asana, pranayam, and concentration are of particular significance.

2. One should be able to sit in an adopted posture for a minimum of two hours at a stretch. This period will need to be extended up to six or even eight hours for a higher awakening.

3. Intense meditation for long durations is energy exhaustive and can cause mental fatigue. Therefore, a practitioner should monitor the ability and advance in a gradual progression.

4. It is also an energy provider. Due absorption of the energy will require a robust and healthy

body. A weak body-mind combination can inflict self-damage.

5. To awaken each chakra, (it has to be in order from the bottom to the top) the focus has to be on the respective location of the chakra. The practitioner has to choose the right spot.

**In nutshell, it must be asserted that meditation is almost the beginning of the end of yoga. It is unrealistic, unprofessional and even harmful that many enthusiasts look at it as a starting point.**

# SAMADHI

The culmination of meditation is *Samadhi*. The union of the consciousness (subject) with the object (of focus) is *Samadhi*.

*'Tadeva artha matra nirvasam swarup sunyam iva samadhih.'*

Patanjali, Sutra III.3

*Tadeva*: means the same, here it refers to Dhyan, meditation.

*Artha*: means the object (of focus).

*Matra*: means only.

*Nirvasam*: means to shine.

*Svarup*: means the form (of the self).

(Here the consciousness of the seeker, the subject, represents the self).

*Sunyam*: means cypher, zero.

(It refers to the complete merger of the self with the object. The self becomes zero).

*Iva*: means that is

*Samadhi*: state of mind with total spiritual absorption.

Meaning of the *sutra*:

When the subject and the self are fully absorbed by the object (of meditation) and awareness becomes non-existent, the subject is in the state of **Samadhi.**

With uninterrupted, intense and prolonged meditation (in the initial stages it may require longer hours of up to ten hours at a stretch), the subject, the seeker acquires the form and identity of the sought, the object. Here consciousness ceases, serenity prevails, awareness of place, space and time also cease and the soul is at the edge of liberation. All the sensual perceptions, memory, imprints of events stand dissolved. It is also referred to as a state of involution. Only silence prevails and submission to God is total. The moment of knowing the true self, the atman (soul), gets nearer but remains uncertain. Till then let us try to understand the meaning and identity of true self-the *atman*.

There are three common ways to establish the identity of a matter and mass. These are:

-Appearance, name and colour

Any of the above alone will not be sufficient to establish a specific identity. All the three together appear to be the sufficient and necessary conditions to establish the identity of an object or species. In cases where semblance is identical, additional information becomes necessary. These will include the nature and properties of the objects under a given condition.

How do we identify the true self? Does the true self possess a geometrical dimension? Does it have a mass and a colour? What are the elements that constitute the self? If none of these identifiable characteristics is relevant, then what is the alternative way? We have the five gross elements constituting the gross body. These elements are earth, water, fire, air, and ether (called *akash* in Sanskrit). These are also referred to as '*panch mahabhuta*'. Add to these the subtle elements of mind, intellect and ego. These are the material (lower) forms of the Creator. All of these can be cognitively identified using the principles of name, colour, and appearance. But there is also a more subtle and higher form (nature) of the Creator that is within us. It is called the spiritual nature in the form of *jiva* (the life force). The following verses from the *Gita* reveal the character of His Lower and Higher nature.

> *Bhumiapoanalo vayuh,kham mano budhhieva cha,*
> 
> *Ahankar itiyam me bhinna prakriti asthadha*
> 
> Verse 4, chapter 7.
> 
> *Apara itah anyam prakritim vidhhi me param,*
> 
> *Jiva bhutam mahabaho yaya idam dharyate jagat*
> 
> Verse 5, Chapter 7.

*Bhumi*: means earth. *Ap*: means water.

*Anal*: means fire.     *Vayu*: means air.

*Kham*:means ether.   *Man*: means mind.

*Budhhih*: means 'intellect'.   *Eva*:means and or also..

*Ch*: means and .     *Iti*: means so.

*Iyam*:   means this or these.

*Me*:     means my.

*Asthadhabhinna*:       means eightfold.

*Prakriti*:       means nature.       *Iyam*: means to assert.

*Apara*:  means lower nature of God.

*Mahabaho*: means brave, warrior par excellence, one way to address Arjun.

*Anyam*: means the other.

*Yaya*:means the cause, the source.

*Idam*: means this (entire).

*Jagat*: means the universe.

*Dharyate*: means to sustain.

*Jivabhutam*: means the life force or principles of life itself.

*Param*:   means   higher,   refers   to   cosmic consciousness.

*Prakritim*: means nature.

*Vidhhih*: means know.

Meaning of the combined verses is as below:

Addressing Arjun, Lord Krishna says, 'my complete nature is divided into two parts. One is my eightfold (material) nature manifested in the form of earth, water, fire, sky and ether. Add to it the mind, intellect and ego. This is my lower (material) nature. The other part of my nature is by which the entire universe is created and sustained. This is my higher (spiritual) nature (the life force, jeevabhutam).

The eight categories, earth, water, fire, air, ether, mind, intellect, and ego are the cause of the following fifteen:

- The five objects of senses: sound, sight, smell, touch, and taste.

- The five senses of perception: ears, eyes, nose, skin, and tongue.

- The five organs of action: the mouth (speech), the feet, the hands, the anus, and the genitals.

The whole of the objective world has been referred to as *jagat* (the Universe). It is the manifestation of the lower nature (*apara prakriti*). This objective or the material world cannot be self-sustaining. The *jivatma* what we call as subjective consciousness (life force) is the sustainer of the objective world. This conscious life force has also been referred to as *purush* and *ksetrajna* (knower of the field, the body).

*Idam shariram kounteya kshetram iti abhidhiyate,*

*Etaddyo vetti tam prahuh kshetryagya iti tadvidah.*

Gita

Verse 1, chapter 13

*Idam*: means 'this'.

*Shariram*: means 'body'.

*Kounteya*: refers to Arjun, son of Kunti.

*Kshetram*: means 'field'.

*Abhidiyate*: means 'known, termed'.

*Etat*: means 'it.'

*Yah*: means 'who'.

*Tam*: means 'him'.

*prahu*: speak of.

*ksetryagya iti*: one with the knowledge of the field (with all its gross and subtle objects), knower of the field.

*Tadvidah*: means 'knowing the truth'

**Meaning of the verse:**

Addressing Arjun as Kounteya (son of Kunti) Krishna says, "This body (with all its gross and subtle elements) is a field. One who has the complete knowledge of it is termed by the discerning sages as *ksetrajna* (knower of the field).

The verse begins with the words '*Idam sariram*'-'this body'. Whose body is it? Who is addressing it? The body by nature is an object. Therefore, there ought to be an owner, a subject of the object. The body is the veil, the cover, the house in which the owner resides. Who is dwelling under the various layers we have described earlier? The body has an end, it dies. Does the dweller also die? Till such time that ego dominates and '*idam sariram*' means 'I am I', we shall remain in a flux of the natural world. Afflictions and sufferings will be our companions. Our conscious mind will remain under the wrap of ignorance. Through yogic practices, this ignorance of ego vanishes and 'I' becomes 'Him'; *Aham tatwam asi* (I am within you). Here 'I' is the Brahman. This is the verse that a teacher narrates to his student in response to the student's anxiety of establishing his identity with the self. It begins with 'tatwam asi' and ends with *Aham brahmashmi* (Though am I). By now, it should be obvious as to who the owner is. Is it the indestructible soul, the '*aksara purusa*' (the conscious self), or the para prakriti (the *jivatma*)? These are several names of one supreme, eternal, timeless, and boundless power sustaining the objective universe. The seeker of the truth, the *sadhaka*, the individual consciousness is relentless in the process to realise the nature of *para prakriti* (the cosmic consciousness). *Patanjali Ashtha Yoga* lays down the process and the procedure to know the Ultimate. There is no guarantee though.

We have extensively used the word consciousness in our various explanations. Like the soul dwelling under the cover of the body and other veils, consciousness lies under the cover of mind. Understanding of the mind and its qualities will be of value.

## Mind and its Qualities

The mind is unsteady and fiery. It mostly relates to the external world through the senses. Its judgement is often instinctive and occasionally with a problematic outcome. Ordinary to extreme pains and pleasures are derived from the actions initiated by the instinctive mind. Yoga says that only through disciplining of the mind, gradual process of detachment, and increasing awareness can one avoid or control the extreme pleasure and pain scenario.

The movement between pleasure and pain is generally referred to as mood swings. In Sanskrit, we call it *chitta vritti*. The cause of these fluctuations can be attributed to the five states of consciousness. These are: based on knowledge, called *pramana* (proof), based on ill-informed or wrong knowledge (*viparyay*), based on imagined situation called fantasy (*vikalpa*), based on memory of past events and actions (*smriti*), and dormant or sleeping state (*nidra*). These are the natural states of consciousness we all pass through from time-to-time. Question will be the relevance of these in yoga. Other than the one based on knowledge all other states can be dangerous. Our state of consciousness determines our action and pattern of behaviour in society. Imagine someone living in fantasy or sleeping mode or reacting in response to memories. The conduct of such a person will be erratic and harmful to society and the self. Yoga practices enable a dream free sound sleep, keeps the mind alert, and under check and most importantly, lives in the moment (the perpetual present). A controlled and healthy mind can discriminate between right and wrong, between reality and fantasy, and use memories for a meaningful present.

## The Body

Patanjali considers the body to be an object and a (destructible) field. All actions, experiments, and experiences are within the body. The senses of perception and organs of action are the sensors and the tools. The mind and intellect determine the level of commitment. The goal is spiritual freedom through 'cessation of movement in the consciousness.'

Stages 1 to 3 of Patanjali Yoga that is, *Yama*, *Niyam*, and *Asana* take care of the physical fitness. Without it, one can never move forward and despite these, one may find the advance journey difficult. Each stage is as important as the previous one. These are complementary and interwoven like a piece of cloth with different kinds and qualities of thread.

Step 4. *Pranayam*. Is the vital link between the gross body and the subtle body. *Pranayam* also provides much-needed energy to the entire body system. It improves endurance ability. Deep pranayam is a prelude to *dharana* (concentration). Sage Swatmarma (15th century saint) believed the control of breath to be the beginning of the control of the mind. He went to the extent of saying and I quote,

'*Teen Lok Ki Sampada, Ek Sans sum Nahi.*'

*Teen* is three.

*Lok* is the Universe.

*Ki* means 'to possess'.

*Sampada* means 'wealth.'

*Sum* is 'equal'.

*Nahi* means 'negation', No.

According to the Hindu belief, there are three universes (*lok*). These are named *swarga lok* (Abode of Gods), planet earth, *prithvi lok* (abode of humans and other species) and hell (abode of cursed species including humans).

**Meaning of the verse is:**

The combined wealth of all the three universes cannot equate to one breath.

The simple interpretation is that breath is life. Life is consciousness. Loss of breath is the loss of consciousness. Loss of consciousness is the loss of life. Under such a situation, the material wealth of any magnitude and variety is meaningless. Thus, breath is the most valuable wealth that cannot be matched with the combined wealth of the three universes.

Steps 5. *Pratyahar*

*Pratyahar* is the synthesis of two words, *prati* and *ahar*. *Prati* means to relinquish or to renunciate. *Ahar* means food. Renunciation of the food of the senses is *pratyahar*. Senses of perception cause desire. Mind through the cognition of the desire causes disturbance in thought. Invariably it stimulates action to fulfil the desire. In the absence of conscious control of senses, the chain of desire multiplies over time. Vision, sound, touch, form, and taste are the food of the senses of perception. Fulfilling these desires is the task of the organs of action. Superfluous material possession and excessive consumption, together with unfulfilled desires cause stress and affliction. Conscious and continuous practice of yoga matures the mind. The matured mind controls the senses. Control of the senses through non-cognition of objects (mind control) is *pratyahar*. Natural aversion to material possession and healthy loss of appetite sets in. When to eat, what to eat, and how much to eat becomes part of nature. Physical and mental afflictions are reduced.

Steps 6 and 7 are crucial. Having perfected 1 to 6, the practitioner is physically well equipped with the right level of stamina and endurance to advance his journey. The arduous task of prolonged and intense concentration is involved. The conscious effort of cessation of mind movement is the goal.

*'Chittavritti nirodhah.'*

Patanjali, Sutra 2.

*Chitta*: is consciousness.

*Vritti*: is flitting nature of mind.

*Nirodh*: is to restrain, to stop, stillness.

To bring the *chitta* to a state of stillness is (one of) the aim (of yoga).

Defining *chitta* is not easy. The nearest literal translation is consciousness. *Chitta* is the repository of all actions, perceptions, emotions, vices, and virtues (physical, intellectual, or spiritual), all vibrations and vibes. Often words like *chitta*, mind, thought, intelligence, intellect, and consciousness are construed as one. These are all subtle in nature. Clarity comes with the advanced practice of yoga. In the final stages, individual consciousness is merged with cosmic consciousness. *Chitta* or cosmic consciousness has been explained in the verse form in Appendix 3 under the title, 'song of the soul.'

Consciousness primarily has three tasks: cognition, conation, and motion. We can call these as recognition, desire, and action. Yoga helps to understand the mechanism of functioning of these tasks. Once we understand the working mechanism, control of functioning becomes easy. By the time a seeker has perfected the art of deep meditation, the knowledge of all functions, from the gross body to the mind sheath are clearly seen and understood. The practitioner can now start the act of control and cessation of *chitta*. It begins with momentary cessation. Continued practice leads to prolonged cessation. Deep meditation leads to *samadhi*, and deep *samadhi* converts cessation into total silence. Silence with serenity is felt. In the initial stage, the duration of realisation of total silence is infinitesimally short. This can be as short as fraction of a momen. As the intensity and duration of the sadhana/meditation increases, so do the duration of the state of silence.

From meditation to a state of *samadhi*, the duration of meditation will need to grow longer and longer. Meditation with high intensity sustained over a long period of time leads to *samadhi*. With continued practise, it forms part of nature. The *sadhaka* then can get into *samadhi* state at will, effortlessly. On the contrary, at the initial stage, the duration of *sadhana* is stated to last up to 10 hours per sitting.

Often, curiosity runs deep on the gains of meditation and *sadhana*. Questions are also asked on the method of validation of these gains. We have already mentioned about the state of the serenity of silence and the ability to transcend time and space.

The vision and power of an enlightened soul can be divine in nature, though there will always be a difference in spread, duration, and nature of divinity. This will be a separate subject by itself. Some inference can be drawn at the concluding stage of the book. Right now, we shall try to address the issue of validation.

There are four established methods to validate a statement. These are:

- Guess (*anuman*)
- Knowledge (*gyan*, empirical or through established sources)
- Experiment (*vigyan*, based on scientific observation and experiment)
- Spiritual awareness (*pragyan*)

Of the four methods of validation mentioned above, the first three, *anuman*, *gyan*, and *vigyan* do not need elaborate explanation. *Anuman* is based on past events and experiences, instinctive or even pure intuition.

*Gyan* is more definitive and always refers to an established record of events described in written form or through other methods of painting, sculpture, mathematical models, etc.

*Vigyan* is pure science. It refers to the knowledge based on collective confirmation of events. It has a predictable theory of cause and effect. All actions under pre-set conditions must produce the same and similar reaction. We see the application of this theory of science in our everyday life, be it healthcare, education, transportation, infrastructure, space exploration, etc.

## Pragyan (Spiritual Awareness).

Our interface with this method of validation is rare. We shall try and give a little more space and time to understand *pragyan*. In our routine life two things play key role. First one is the sense perception. Our initial knowledge of things and events is pure sense perception. The mind carries the impression of these perceptions and uses it as a memory for reflection. In addition to the memory, there is intelligence which can analyse the perceived information and initiate action. Action will always have options of 'to do' or 'not to do.' Duality becomes the guiding principle of life. Duality explained in Hindi will mean '*dubhida*,' being uncertain. The root cause of uncertainty is ignorance or incomplete knowledge. Perception by its limitations is imperfect. On a bright sunny day, we perceive the sky and the ocean perfect blue. In reality, we know that both are colourless. Perception of blue is wrong, yet valid. Those who know the truth will be able to unveil the cause of the duality. Truth harbours no duality.

The second feature that governs our routine life pattern is the freedom of will. In more common socio-political terms, it is also referred to as the freedom of choice. There is apparently nothing new in this. Freedom is an essential part of life. As we progress in our yogic accomplishment, our physical and intellectual abilities, our vigour and strength, our stamina all get a boost in their respective potentials. As we have seen in the duality of action, a similar situation arises when there is freedom of will or choice. It is a sign of wavering, unstable mind. As one advances in yogic pursuit, there is clarity in the working of the various body sheaths (layers engulfing the true self, the *purush*, the soul). When clarity sets in, the concept of freedom alters. Instead of **seeking 'freedom of will' we look for 'will to be free.'** The desire to will to be free is the starting point of *pragyan*. At this point, the intelligence serving the senses gradually shifts the direction of the journey from 'in to out' to 'out to in.' This journey from 'out to in' is spiritual intelligence. As intelligence moves from 'out to in' the nature of resultant awareness becomes clear and free from duality. The awareness of this nature is referred to as *pragyan*. Freedom of will based on sense perception is the pristine nature of the animal world. On the other hand, the 'will to be free' is the goal of spiritual intelligence (*pragyan*). This goal is attainable through an intense inward journey. The process of this intense journey is the *sadhana* of *samadhi*, the highest quality of meditation. The knowledge revealed during this process is *pragyan*.

As the 'out to in' journey begins the practitioner gets the full and clear understanding of each of the five sheaths engulfing the real self, the soul. The darkness caused by these sheaths fades in the light of awareness. The vision of the practitioner gets clearer and brighter with the unveiling of each sheath. Finally, the seeker is face-to-face with the seer, the unblemished pure soul shining in its own light. One is supposedly said to be in the state of *samadhi*. In this state, duality vanishes and the truth is revealed. The practitioner has attained divine wisdom. But freedom is still far. On freedom, Sri B.K.S. Iyengar in his book, *Light on Life*, writes and I quote:

"To a yogi, freedom implies not being battered by the dualities of life, its ups and downs, its pleasures, and its suffering. It implies equanimity and ultimately that there is an inner serene core of one's being that is never out of touch with the unchanging eternal infinite."

The practitioner has reached the state of conscious awareness about the existence of the soul. It stimulates the instinct to be free. But the soul is still in the cage. The soul itself is a non-physical reality. Acceptance or dismissal of the reality of the soul is spontaneous till it is self-realised.

This is how Saint Kabir, the Sufi saint and poet of the 15th century described it:

*Dus dware ka pinjara,*

*Tame panchhi ek,*

*Awat ko acharaj nahi,*

*Jaye to acharaj hoi*

*Dus* is ten

*Dwar* is gate

*Ka* is of

*pinjara* is cage

*tame* is therein

*panchhi* is bird

*ek* is one

*awat* is coming in

*acharaj* is wonder, astonishment

*nahi* is not

*jaye* is gone

Meaning of the verse:

In the above poem, Saint Kabir refers to the body as a cage with ten gates. These gates are the nine openings (two eyes, nostrils, ears, and one mouth, anus, genital, and one being the top of the head. *Panchhi* (bird) refers to the soul. The literal meaning is that in this body (cage) of ten gates the soul (bird) resides. The arrival is unnoticed, and the stay of the soul (bird) is unrecognised till it departs. Why? Why should there be astonishment on the departure of the bird when the arrival was unnoticed? It is strange that we identify life with the soul when it is gone. The departure of the soul is the death of the body. By deduction, it would mean that the soul enters the body with the birth. We shall see.

How and when does the soul enter the body? Does the soul have a lifetime? What is the abode of the soul? It is well accepted that the departure of the soul is death to the body. Some believe that the soul enters the body at the time of birth. Is the birth of body inception of the soul? According to Swami Yogeswaranand Saraswati (refer his book, *Science of Soul*), the entry of the soul in the body coincides with the contact of the sperm (*shukra*) with the ovum (*raja*). When the sperm joins the ovum, a small mass of flesh (*morula*) is formed in the womb of the mother. Simultaneously *jiva*, the individual soul, enters the embryo. All other basic elements, some derived from the cosmic consciousness and some from the mother, assume the shape of an oval mass. In the centre of this mass resides the soul. Though it is confined in a compact space it has complete freedom to escape from any part it chooses to. The departure of the soul is death to the body. This is what happens even in the unfortunate instances of abortion. It establishes that the soul leaves with the death of the body, but it enters with the formation of *morula* when the sperm meets the ovum. This unseen, unrecognised and unmanifested entity called the soul is the essence of life. It is said to be the support base of all activities of resultant pains and pleasures, gains and loss, success, and failure. It is the one that identifies with the Supreme Soul often expressed as, *Aham tatwam asi* (I, the Supreme dwell within you). One who lives with the conscious realisation of the soul within is free from the dualities of the physical world. But the soul is still in the cage looking for complete freedom, liberation. In yoga, sadhana of samadhi is the way forward to liberation.

In the earlier chapters, we have been able to establish the sheaths or layers engulfing the inner self.      These are:

*Annamaya Kosh* (gross body sheath).

*Pranmaya Kosh* (energy sheath).

*Manomaya Kosh* (mind sheath).

*Gyanmaya Kosh* (intelligence sheath) .

These sheaths are with the human body from the time of birth and live with it till death. The gross body sheath is visible. The other sheaths are subtle in nature and not visible to the naked eyes. Through yoga, one can see the form and colour of these invisible subtle sheaths. Each of these sheaths is also identified with their respective energy characteristics. These are:

- *Sarir Shakti*: Power of the body.
- *Pran Shakti*: Power of *pran* (life force).
- *Soch Shakti*: Thought power.
- *Gyan Shakti*: Power of knowledge.

*Sarir Shakti*, power of the body can easily be qualified and quantified. It can be felt and manifested too. It can be equated to *annamaya* sheath.

*Pran Shakti* is subtle in nature. It is responsible to keep the body cells, the subatomic particles, the organs, and the overall system in healthy condition. The radiance of this energy will reflect as an aura of an individual. This can be equated to *pranmaya* (energy) sheath.

Thought power can be termed as the power of mind control. It is still more subtle in nature. The energy emanating from such a person can cause vibration and create positive vibes. It can also work as a defence mechanism against negative vibes. It needs no medium to travel. The intuitive power and memory of such a person are exceptional. This can be equated to *manomaya* sheath.

*Gyan Shakti* is an advanced state of thought power. It is the power of the intellect. *Gyan Shakti* has added advantage of cosmic awareness. It can do all that thought power does with greater intensity and consistency. It can cause to see through time and space.

*Sarir Shakti* consumes energy derived basically from the food we eat and drinks we take. It also derives energy from the oxygenated blood. *Pran Shakti* gets the energy through breath and the life force (*pran*) present in the cosmos. These two kinds of energies are useful in keeping the two related sheaths in a healthy and robust condition. These also work as a protection against physical afflictions.

The other two energies are extremely powerful. Whereas the related sheaths are preserved through the energy derived from life forces the innate energy of their own is invariably scattered with the rapid movement of mind, thought, and *chitta*. Bringing back these scattered thoughts to one point can produce an energy impact of a huge dimension. It is like the sunlight. If we capture the sunlight through a convex lens, the heat energy content of converging beams on the other side is many times more powerful compared to the rays entering the lens.

A seeker equipped with these extraordinary energy packs is now in an advanced stage of his final leg of the journey to enlightenment. Why do we need these packs? We can well compare it to the journey in the physical world. In context to the world of the phenomenon, one needs to be in a sound healthy condition before embarking on a long journey. One is also expected to carry some logistical emergency support system to meet the challenges of any emergency. The other feature of any journey is the **movement** from point A to point B. It can also be from point B to A, or any other direction, linear, circular or irregular.

In the spiritual world, the journey involves no physical movement. It is a journey from the physical self, the *annamaya kosh* to *anandmaya* (blissful) *kosh*. It is a journey from 'out to in'. It employs no outside vehicle. If one reaches the destination, there is no provision of a return journey. One can choose to return from any intermediate station but not after reaching the destination. The reason is simple. As soon as the practitioner unveils the blissful sheath, all the other sheaths are dissolved. Only the blissful sheath remains. The spiritual journey starts from the gross body and passes through stages given below:

Gross body (*Annamay Kosh*)→ *Pranmaya kosh* (energy sheath) →*Manomay kosh* (mind sheath)→intelligence *kosh* (*Gyanmaya* sheath)→*Anandmaya kosh* (bliss sheath)

During intense meditation, the seeker can witness the status and functioning of all the sheaths and their constituents. The light which was dormant, hidden in a cave, is now in the open, lighting the entire system. Colour and intensity of the lights will be different at different stages. It is assumed to be the brightest but soothing and pure white in colour when cosmic consciousness is realised. The practitioner will be endowed with the divine vision. **The seeker can see the events of the past and the future. He will be able to witness the blissful and enthralling finite form of the infinite God. In the process, he will also witness all the acts and events in their true nature. Some of these can be most horrifying and destructive with the entire**

**creation engulfed by fire of terrifying nature and magnitude. It can cast a disturbing and harmful effect on weak and ill-equipped individuals.** An instance in the *Bhagavad Gita*, the Holy book of the Hindus will make this assertion abundantly clear.

A great war was fought in the year 3138 B.C. It was a family feud resulting in a war of all India dimension. Almost all the kings and kingdoms of the time were involved in the war. Some records say 1.6 billion people lost their lives. The war was fought at Kurushetra approximately 150 kilometres away from present-day Delhi. The principal architect of the war was Lord Krishna. He had vowed not to use any instrument of war Himself. However, He agreed to be the charioteer of Arjun, a great warrior, acclaimed devotee, and cousin of Lord Krishna. Lord Krishna is the incarnate of Lord Vishnu and is worshipped throughout the faithful Hindu community as the Supreme Godhead.

During those days the instruments and appliances used for war were bows and arrows, mace, swords, and spears. The army construct was of foot soldiers, warriors on horses, elephants, and chariots. The war was fought at a close distance including physical fights except for the ones with bows and arrows. Before the start of the war and conches were blown (as an affirmation to start the war), Arjun got into a serious dilemma. He doubted the rationality of the war involving family, friends, gurus, and relations. Was the war worthwhile? Can a victory gained by killing those who should be revered, respected, and loved be worthwhile a celebration? Will such a victory not bring more pain and affliction? Arjun wanted to see the two army formations from close and equidistance. He humbly urged Krishna to pull the chariot in the centre of the two lined up armies. Krishna pulled the reins of the horses and took the chariot in the centre of the battlefield. Arjun made a survey of the rival army formation. He was stunned. He saw the grandfather in whose lap he had spent his childhood and one who was his idol. He saw his reverend teacher at whose feet he had learnt the skills of war. He saw his cousins, friends, and relations and thousands of soldiers. He fell into self-doubt. His body was shivering in despair. His will to fight was dwindling. He dropped his famous Gandive (name of his bow) and sat on the chariot dejected. He expressed his desperate physical and mental condition to Krishna and questioned the rationality of the war.

Thus started the eternal teaching and preaching of the Lord to extricate Arjun from the mirage of his cowardly thinking. The battlefield of Kurukshetra was to witness the defining moments of learning the essence of human existence. The philosophy of life, *karma* (duty), *dharma* (righteousness), *bhakti*, and yoga was expounded by the Knower and Creator of all things and all knowledge. Krishna proclaimed that

He was the origin and end of all things and all events from eternity to eternity. He emphasised that the war was the need of the time. He also advised that to fight the war was Arjun's personal, social, moral, and ethical duty. A lengthy discourse ensued between Lord Krishna and Arjun. A record of the discourse was first mentioned by Sage Ved Vyas in his epic book titled *Mahabharat* in which the full text of the dialogue has been recorded. The teaching at the battlefield part was later published separately under the title *Bhagavad Gita* also referred to as *Gita*. The long discourse was in the form of questions and answers. It spanned 700 verses. Arjun's illusion, his self-doubt and dilemma were cleared but not entirely. He still entertained one illusion. It concerned real Nature and Form of Lord Krishna. Arjun was convinced of the Divinity in Krishna. He wanted validation. He prayed if the Lord would be pleased and be kind to show him (Arjun) His (Krishna's) real form. What followed has been elucidated below in the form of questions and answers. It must be noted that the whole dialogue was in Sanskrit. No matter how well we translate, the spirit of the original expression will be missing. The readers will bear me out.

Arjun: Prays as below;

'Manyase yadi tat shakyam,

Maya drashtum iti Prabho,

Yogeshwar tato me twam,

Darshaya atmanam abyayam.'

                          Gita, Verse 4, chapter 11.

*prabho*: way to address the lord, the God.

*Yadi:* means if.

*Maya:* is me.

*Tat:* is that.

*Drashtum:* means to see.

*Shakyam:* means possible.

*Iti:* is so.

*Twam:* is you.

*Manyase:* means think.

*Yogeswar:* refers to the Lord of yoga, Krishna.

*atmanam* :means the( imperishable) form.

*abyayam* is imperishable

The complete meaning of the verse will read something like this;

O Yogeswar (God of yoga)! if you think I can see Your imperishable Form then reveal the same to me.

Krishna replies:

"Pashya me Parth roopani,

shatshah ath sahahastra sah,

nanavidhani divyani,

nanavarnakritin chah."

Gita, Verse5, ch.11

*Pashya:* is to behold.

*Me:* is me.

*Rupani:* is forms.

*Shatshah:* is hundreds.

*Sahastre:* is thousands.

*Nanavidhani:* is multifarious.

*Divyani:* is divine.

*Nanavarnakritin:* means varying colours and forms.

Meaning of the verse:

Lord Krishna says, O Parth! At present behold hundreds and thousands of My Divine forms in various colour and shapes. Krishna further says,

"Ih ekastham jagat kritnam,

pashya adya sacharacharam,

mum dehe Gudakesh,

yat anyat drashtum ikshashi."

Verse 7, ch.11

The Lord goes on to say: Behold within me the entire creation of animate and inanimate beings and everything else that you wish to see.

Arjun was still ensnared within and sought to see the true expanded cosmic form of God.

Krishna conceded to show His Cosmic Form. But Arjun would not be able to witness or withstand the brilliance and nature of the Cosmic Form with his human eyes. The good Lord granted Arjun divine vision and revealed His supremely glorious, universal expanded form.

Arjun saw the supreme deity with many mouths and eyes, adorned with divine ornaments and weapons. He saw multiple hands and stomach, multiple faces and eyes on all sides with infinite dimension. The form displayed, had no beginning and no end nor had middle. The brilliance of the light emanating was akin to the effulgence of a thousand suns shining at the same time. The universe and entire creation could be seen within the space of His mouth. Arjun was simply wonderstruck with the impossible happenings. He made his submission with total surrender and thus he said,

*'Pashyami devam teva dev dehe sarwantatha*
*bhut visheshsanghyan,Brahnanmisham kamalasanastham*
*rishin cha sarwan*
*urgan cha divyan'.*

*Verse 15, ch. 11*

I see you endowed with numerous arms, bellies, mouths, and eyes. I do not see the beginning, the end and centre of your form. I find the entire universe is filled with you.

In addition to all the exciting and wondrous things, Arjun saw the scariest event taking place. He saw the universal destruction. He saw the frightening teeth and flare of fire causing this destruction.

Arjun found most of the warriors and soldiers ready for war at Kurukshetra making their last journey and entering the scary jaws of the Supreme. Arjun was frightened. In obeisance, he prayed if the Lord would be pleased to return to His human form. And the Lord obliged.

This little extract from the *Gita* can be interpreted in many ways. My interpretations are two. Firstly, the yoga practitioner should appreciate the severity of harm one could cause to the self by **casual meditation** without mastering the art of *yama*, *niyama*, *asana*, *pranayam*, *pratyahar*, and *dharana*. Divinity is not all bliss. It is also associated with horror acts of unprecedented nature and magnitude causing death and destruction.

The second one is a realisation of the sense of cosmic consciousness. In that state of mind, one can see the universe and all events of past, present, and future. The seeker transcends time and space. He is liberated and is free to move in higher spaces and other universes at will. He is totally free from the bondage of all the sheaths. In the spiritual world, we call it *kaivalya*. Patanjali last sutra defines it as below:

*'Purushartha shunyanam,*

*gunanam pratiprasavah,*

*Kayvalyam swarup pratishtha va,*

*chitti shakti itih.'*

*Purushartha*: *Karmas* one must do as a human. These are:

*Dharma* (to learn, understand, and follow the path of righteousness),

*Artha* (application of skill and knowledge to create value and wealth),

*Kam* (fulfilment of natural demands and desires of senses),

*Moksha* (acts leading to liberation, individual soul joining the Supreme soul).

*Sunyanam*: discount to zero.

*Gunanam*: The three *gunas* that control and define time and all activities. These are:

*Sattva:* (thought and action pure in nature, society governed by knowledge and wisdom free from vices. Good for all).

*Rajo:* (thought and actions in favour of a few chosen ones. Good for self plus favoured few).

*Tamo:* (defines malice and prejudices, arrogance with ignorance, dull mind with little or no action. Good for the self alone).

*Pratiprasvah***:** A kind of involution in spiritual word. Return to the original state.

*Kaivalyam***:** Freedom from all bondage, the liberation of the soul.

*Pratishtha***:** Located, established identity.

*Chütishakti***:** Power of consciousness.

*Iti***:** That is all, the end.

Our life can be evaluated based on the *purusharthas* (our *karmas*), the quality of the *karmas* under the categorization of the *gunas* and finally our spiritual effort for the liberation of the soul. In the above sutra, Sage Patanjali has enunciated the final act and state of the soul on the verge of liberation. The nearest possible translation will be somewhat like this:

When one has done all the *purusharthas* (*karmas*) as described above,

When one has transcended all the *gunas*,

When one has returned all the *karmas* and *gunas* to where it came from (state of *sunya* or nothingness, no thought, no ego, and no desire),

When the consciousness is clearly established in the image of the real self,

When the seeker and the seer become one, that is the state of *kaivalya*-total liberation or *moksha*.

It is a state of non-being transformed into being. It is referred to as *nirbij samadhi*.

There is an interesting story relating to Sri. Ramkrishna Paramhans, the great spiritual master of the 19th century and *guru* of Swami Vivekanand. He had the ability to get into *samadhi* at will. It had become part of his nature. But his *samadhi* was always focussed and devoted to goddess Kali. One day, a travelling *Vedic* monk came to the temple where Ramakrishna lived. After a brief conversation, the monk told Ramkrishna that he (Ramkrishna) could go beyond his current level of attainment. He asked Ramkrishna to get into *samadhi*. Since the state of *samadhi* had become part of Ramkrishna's nature, in a short time he got into the *samadhi* mode. The monk picked a shard of broken glass and mercilessly pierced in between the eyebrows of Ramkrishna. Ramkrishna felt terrible pain. He also felt a change in his spiritual bliss. He felt that within himself he has killed goddess Kali and entered the state of *nirbij samadhi*. He found himself in a void, the final state of oneness with the self. He was totally free having attained the ultimate goal of yoga.

Interestingly, the frequently asked question is, can all who follow the path of yoga attain *kaivalya*, *moksha*? The following two quotes from the two popular religious Hindu epics provide the answer.

*'Manushyanam sahastrayeshu kashchit yatati sidhaye,*

*Yatatamapi sidhanam kashit mam vetti tatvatah.'*

Gita, verse 3, chapter 7.

*Manushyanam*: means men.

*Sahastrayeshu*: means thousands.

*Kashchit*: means hardly one.

*Yatati*: means effort.

*Sidhye*: means to achieve, to succeed.

*Yattam*: amongst those.

*Sidhanam*: refers to Yogis striving for liberation.

*Api*: means again.

*Mam*: means Me (refers to God).

*Vetti*: To know.

*Tatvatah*: True form and nature of (God).

Meaning of the verse: Amongst thousands of men rarely one strives to know about Me and amongst thousand striving souls one (who has totally surrendered unto Me) shall be able to know My true Form and Nature.

*'Soi jane jehu dehu janai,*

*Janat Tumahi Tumahi hoi jai.'*

From Tulsi krit, Ramcharit Manas

*Soi*: Addressing one pursuing the path of spiritual awareness.

*Janai*: means to apprise.

*Jehu*: means to whom.

*Janai*: means to reveal.

*Janat*: means to know

*Tumahi*: refers to You, The God.

*Hoi*: means to happen.

*Jai*: means done.

Meaning of the verse is: Of all those striving to know Me, only he would know upon whom is My Grace. One who knows Me, becomes Me.

Thus far we have seen that acts of *Japa* (chanting), *tap* (penance), *tyag* (renunciation), *gyan* (knowledge), *bhakti* (devotion), and yoga may have their spiritual attainments. However, the right to *moksha* (liberation of soul) depends on the quality of surrender and Grace of God. Total liberation is possible only with *sattvik samadhi* where no desire exists. A verse from the *Gita* states:

*'Dhrittya yaya dharayate manah pranendriyakriya,*

*Yogenvyabhicharinya dhrit sa Parth sattvaki'*

Meaning of the verse is: Addressing Arjun as Parth the Lord says, "one who through the practice of yoga has earned firm control on his mind, the vital airs (life force) and the senses is *sattvik* by nature." Liberation for such a person is imminent.

In the subsequent verse no. 34, it is stated that those still saddled with the desires and acts of *dharma* (righteousness), *artha* (wealth), and *kam* (gratification of senses), will have limited freedom for a pre-determined time. These are *rajashi* in nature with a carry-forward option to the next life.

There is yet another lot suffering from evil thoughts and mind. These are *tamasi* in nature. *Moksha* for such a person is far distant.

Yoga is *nishkam karm*. One needs to keep doing it as part of one's duty without expectation of reward, whereas yogic practices can bring firmness and grace to the body, it can bring steadiness to the mind and endurance for meditation. The attainment of the ultimate will depend on the following three final factors:

1. Will and grace of God.
2. State of consciousness (*sattvik, rajashi, tamasi*).
3. Total surrender to God.

# APPENDIX 1

During the course of the *yogabhyasa*, the practitioner will experience unusual sensation, soft vibrations, change in attitude, altered priorities, and numerous other effects as stated below. Such experiences are the natural effects of yoga. These are incidental gains. These only confirm that the practitioner is on the right path. Such gains should not be abused. These can be used only for the benefit of all as defined in, 'Bahujan Sukhaya, Bahujan Hitaya,' meaning, for the good and happiness of all.

1. Hearing of the sound of the eardrums.

2. The clear and appreciable feel of palpitations of the heart and vibration in the nervous system.

3. Fluttering of upper lips and soft crawling vibration along the spine, the face, the arms, and the legs.

4. The vibration of the mind.

5. Healthy loss of appetite.

6. An increasing loss of interest in worldly possessions.

7. Development of vision to see the internal functioning of the body.

8. Ability to bring the body and mind to a state of total silence (non-existence).

9. Control of the three *gunas*: *Sattva*, *Rajo* and *Tamo*.

10. Affliction-free body with grace.

11. Can see through time and space.

12. Is fully aware of the cosmic structure, movement of celestial entities, and their effect.

13. Can see the past and predict the future from eternity to eternity.

14. Develop skills to express and understand all languages ( xenoglossy) including that of animals, birds and plants. (*vaid* Lukman is famous for his conversation with the trees and plants).

15. Ability to transport his astral and gross body at will.

16. Ability to be invisible.

17. Ability to know the nature of past and future lives.

17. Ability to enter others' body and mind.

18. Can levitate.

19. Can create fire at will.

20. Can walk on water and on thorny paths.

21. Can control hunger and thirst.

22. Always at peace with the self, kind, and compassionate to all.

# APPENDIX 2

The ultimate spiritual aim of *Patanjali Astha Yoga* is *Kaivalya* (liberation). This is achieved through deep *Sadhana*. During the process, there are many incidental gains. These have been listed under appendix 1.

One significant achievement prior to *Kaivalya* is *Karma Mukta* and the one beyond it is, *Brahmalin*.

We shall try to understand the difference between the three, i.e., *Mukta*, *Kaivalya* (liberation), and *Brahmalin*.

*Karma Mukta* is being free from the fruits of action. Here, the soul is together with the gross body. The mind or *chitta* is controlled and ego vanishes. *Iswarpranidhan*, a total surrender to God is established.

Liberation: The soul, after leaving the gross body, enjoys absolute freedom. It is free from all kinds of afflictions, ignorance, and pride. It lives in bliss, yet it is not free from the cycle of birth and death. The quality and duration of freedom of liberation are dependent upon the intensity and level of meditation. According to views of some *acharyas* (spiritual Gurus), the following points can help attain liberation:

A. Those who meditate on senses, consider them as the identity of the self. The individual senses merge into cosmic senses. This state of liberation lasts for a period of ten *Manvantaras* (306.72 million years). After having enjoyed the bliss of

liberation for ten Manvantaras, such souls are born again.

B. Those who meditate on the five basic elements, earth, water, fire, air, and space consider them as the identity of the self. This state of liberation lasts for a hundred *Manvantaras* (3.06 billion years), post which, they return to earthly life.

C. Those who win over ego, consider the ego as the identity of the self. Their liberation lasts for a thousand *Manvantaras* (30.6 billion years) at the end of which they return to earthly life.

D. Those who meditate over intellect as the identity of self, their period of liberation lasts for ten thousand *Manvantaras* (306 billion years).

E. Those who meditate on formless, Absolute Brahma do not return to life. The individual soul merges with the Supreme Soul. These are called *Brahmalin*.

*Manvantar* is a unit of time. One *Manvantar* is = 71 *Chaturyug*; I *chaturyuga* =4.32million years. (Total durations have been rounded up).

Culled from Science of Soul.

# APPENDIX 3

## SONG OF THE SOUL -COSMIC CONSCIOUSNESS

I am neither ego nor reason,
I am neither mind nor thought,
I cannot be heard nor cast into words,
Nor by smell nor sight ever caught,
In light and wind I am not found,
Nor yet in earth and sky,
Consciousness and joy incarnate,
Bliss of the blissful am I.

I have no name, I have no life,
I breathe no vital air,
No elements have moulded me,
No bodily sheath in my lair,
I have no speech, no hands, no feet,
No means of evolution,
Consciousness and joy am I,
And bliss in dissolution.

I cast aside hatred and passion,
I conquered delusion and greed,
No touch of pride caressed me,

So envy never did breed,
Beyond all faiths, past the reach of wealth,
Past freedom, past desire,
Consciousness and joy am I,
And bliss is my attire.

Virtue or vice, or pleasure and pain,
Are not my heritage,
No sacred texts, nor offerings,
Nor prayers nor pilgrimage,
I am neither food nor eating,
Nor yet the eater am I,
Consciousness and joy incarnate,
Bliss of the blissful am I.

I have no misgivings of death,
No chasms of death divide me,
No parent ever called me child,
No bond of birth ever tied me,
I am neither disciple nor master,
I have no pen no friend,
Consciousness and joy am I,
And merging in bliss is my end.

Neither knowable, knowledge nor knower am I,
Formless is my form,
I dwell within the senses,
But they are not my home,
Ever serenely balanced,

I am neither free nor bound,
Consciousness and joy am I,
And bliss is where I am found.
Culled from Jiva, Jeevatma, Parmatma
Evam Yoga

# QUANTUM YOGA

### (Energy Concept).

### What is yoga?
Atha Yoga Anushashanam - Patanjali

The above quote, which is also the first sutra (aphorism) of Patanjali Yoga Sutras, means:

Yoga is a discipline. Yoga is also a goal in itself. Yoga is a means. Yoga is Shakti (energy as the nearest English equivalent). Yoga is the cause of the cosmos. Yoga is the whole, omnipresent, and omnipotent. Only through yoga will one be able to understand yoga.

This paper is a brief introduction to the energy aspect of yoga and its role in human evolution and enlightenment.

### What is Energy?
Law of Physics defines energy as the work done over time. It also discovered various forms of energy, their application, and their inter-relationship including the relationship of matter with energy through the most elegant theory in the

world of science, Theory of Relativity, in the early 20th century by Albert Einstein:

$$E = MC^2$$

Where:

E = Energy

M = Mass

C = Speed of light (300,000 kms/sec)

Application of this equation has resulted in the possibility of acquiring access to the much-needed energy for growth and development in the material world. It has also caused the creation of the most destructive weapon, the nuclear bomb.

With each successive scientific revelation, curiosity to know the source of the primal energy and origin of cosmos intrigued the scientific mind. Every time the collective world of Science felt that the answer was in their grasp, the reality receded.

The question related to primal energy and the search for the Absolute truth is also the ultimate goal of the spiritual world, at least in the eastern philosophy of religions.

The similarity ends with the goal. Methodologies are far too different. Science is still struggling with the vision of expanding the universe, empty space, and dark matter on the macro side and the uncertain and unpredictable behaviour of fundamental particles on the micro side.

The Big Bang Theory related to the Time Zero of the universe is not a theory anymore. It is now believed that Space, Time, and Energy already existed.

The Spiritual World starts with a belief of eternity. It also believes in the Omnipresent and the Omnipotent nature of the Supreme. Awareness of, be it the nature and source of Primal Energy or God, is possible only by individual efforts. Each conscious being has the potential to realise the truth if she/he follows the right path.

In his book, *Advaita on Zen and Tao*, R. Balsekar states, 'Primal Energy, functioning through the billions of human beings, produces through each one of them, every instant, whatever is supposed to be produced according to a conceptual cosmic law.'

A somewhat similar statement appears in the book, *Tao Te Ching* by Lao Tzu (a great Chinese philosopher in 6th century BC), when he says, 'As one advances and the intellectual awareness goes deeper it becomes evident that only God's will prevails and that you are never the doer.'

Buddha said, 'Events happen, deeds are done, consequences happen, but there is no individual doer of anything.'

'Everything is predetermined,' said Stephen Hawking.

"Free will is an illusion," said David Bohn

The essence of these short quotes is that life is not what we live, life is lived as designed. That is what we call life as per God's will or the Cosmic law (non-volitional life).

Having accepted the real doer, act we must. The processes of action get reasonable momentum with the external environment and internal awareness. Every action, and every deed one performs, adds up to the journey of life. The most difficult yet, most fascinating part of the life's journey is knowledge of the self.

'Knowledge of the self is the highest knowledge,' writes J. M. Macfie in his book, *Myths and Legends of India*. He further adds, 'The system of yoga reveals the true wisdom.'

The most comprehensive and step-by-step actionable guide to yoga has been explained by the great Indian Sage Patanjali (200-500 BC). These are known as *Patanjali Astha Yoga* describing eight limbs of yoga where each limb prepares the practitioner for the next leading from the gross to the subtle, and finally to the Absolute. These are:

*1. Yama* - Cardinal principles of life for the self

*2. Niyam* - Norms of living (conduct)

*3. Asana* - Posturing for physical fitness

*4. Pranayam* - Physiological fitness and awareness of cosmic energy

*5. Pratyahar* -Self-Restraint (control of desires)

6. *Dharana* -Concentration

7. *Dhyan* - Meditation

8. *Samadhi* - Realisation of the self (state of *Kaivalya* - liberation)

Quantum Yoga and energy concepts revolve around the fourth leg of *Patanjali Astha Yoga*, Pranayam. Pranayam, simply defined, is the art of conscious voluntary breathing. A common understanding of breathing is the inhalation of air, oxygenation of the blood, extraction, and discarding of carbon dioxide Together with air is the acquisition of the vital energy, *Pran*. The goal is acquisition and management of life force -*Pran* through *Ayam*, meaning expansion and extension. Thus, *Pranayam* signifies the acquisition of the cosmic force through the expansion of the lungs and extension of time in a breathing cycle consisting of inhalation, retention, exhalation, and retention. What follows is a short introduction to the Science of the system.

The windpipe which provides the passage for air, in and out of the system is approximately 10 cm long and 2 cm in diameter. It branches further into two primary bronchi connecting the left and right lungs. These, then branch into tiny air carriers known as bronchioles terminating into tiny sacs known as alveoli. These sacs are in clusters and number some 300 million, lining each lung. In a healthy person with average built lungs, when fully expanded and spread, will occupy an area of nearly 70 to 90 sq. metres, almost half the size of a tennis court. This is

45 times the surface area of the average human skin. It is herein the sacs that the exchange of oxygen and carbon dioxide takes place.

The energy carriers in the body carrying blood, air, and fluid consist of nearly 5.6 billion networks measuring some 10,000 kms in length. These networks deliver the required energy to the tiniest constituents of the entire body system. Then there are 40 trillion bacteria, 37 trillion cells, and some 100 billion neurons restless, and scattered. All these constituents and the system/sub-system must regularly get their own share of life force for a healthy, meaningful living. The first objective of *Pranayam* is the acquisition, delivery, and storage of energy.

Energy is acquired in two established ways. First, through the food we eat and digest. Normally, no matter what the nutrient content in food is, only 10 per cent of the content is converted into energy. From the balance, 30 to 40 per cent is consumed in the formation of fat and muscles. The remaining 50 to 60 per cent goes as waste.

The second process of energy acquisition, including the one needed for proper digestion, and other system functions is derived from the cosmic energy through *Pranayam*. We can as well spell it as *Pran* or life force itself. It has been aptly said:

*Teen Lok Ki Sampada, Ek Sans Sum Nahi*

(Translated literally, it means, the combined wealth of the three worlds (*Lok*) cannot match the value of one breath.) Here the three worlds, as referred in Hindu beliefs, are *Swarg*, *Nark*, and *Bhu* (Prithvi) i.e., Heaven, Hell, and Earth.

*Pran* is not just a life force in living entities. It is omnipresent and omnipotent. *Pran* is cosmos as a whole, including its massive and mighty to tiniest and weak components. It is the sum total of all the seen and unseen forces of nature. In living entities, the manifestation of *Pran* is significantly compared to non-living entities.

*Pranayam* is the beginning of the realisation of *Pran*. It also opens the door to the journey ahead, by sublimation of the body, mind, and ego to reach the final destination. One experiences the aura of a self-illumined light, the quality, and intensity of which remains beyond description. Once reached there, there is no more destination nor evolution. Death and life possibly fuse together. There is only Being So described Albert Einstein. Consciousness fully dissolves into the ecstasy of the Light that finally merges with the Universal Energy, which in Hindu religious philosophy is termed as *Brahma*.

Dr Brian Weiss in his book, *Many Lives, Many Masters*, refers to the cosmic energy concept somewhat like this:

The cosmos (besides containing the physical entities) has an energy source that surrounds us and contains the memory of entire human race and all events -from eternity to eternity.

Why is Quantum Yoga the title assigned to this paper? In yoga, we have observed that everything manifested or unmanifested was created by one Primal Energy (Universal or Cosmic *Pran*). What about Science?

Energy in Science

Let us start from three basic circuit diagrams. Fig 1 depicts a simple circuit consisting of a battery (source of energy), a switch, connecting wires, and a lamp. The switch has two positions, open and close. When it is closed, the lamp glows and light is radiated. What really happens is that the uninterrupted movement of electrically charged particles known as electrons along the circuit instantly converts into light energy when it passes through the lamp filament. This is what we observe in our everyday life.

Fig. 2 depicts the operation of a pump used for irrigation. Here, the electrical energy, commonly called electricity, is sourced from the utility operator. The energy in this instance is used to run a motor attached to a pump that delivers water to the farm. Here, the electrical energy is transformed into mechanical energy.

Fig 3. The heat and thermal shock from the explosion of a nuclear device

To an observer, the three diagrams are related to light, water, and heat respectively. Rarely, the focus is on the source of energy enabling these end results, which in themselves are manifestations of energy. This concept of everything as energy was the crux of the quantum mechanics theory that will be touched briefly in paragraphs below.

The 17th century was the century of Isaac Newton, whom Albert Einstein, three hundred years later described as, 'Perhaps the greatest advance in thought that a single individual was ever privileged to make.' Newton gave the revolutionary meaning to Cartesian Theory of Nature as a perfect machine. It was subsequently supported by the great mathematician, scientist, and philosopher, Rene Descartes. The theory of classical physics was well accepted. It believed in the mechanistic and deterministic view of nature, where God did not exist, and the world was like a mechanical clock. It remained unchallenged till the turn of the 20th century that witnessed two great laws in physics:

1. Theory of Relativity
2. The Quantum Mechanics

While the first one relates to the functioning of large distances (inter-planetary distances and the cosmos) and high speed (speed of light at 300,000 km/sec), the second one deals with behavioural patterns of particles at the subatomic level. Though the mechanistic view of classical physics is still valid, in our perceptible known environment that has been termed as the 'zone of middle dimension;' it falls short in offering valid explanation involving interplanetary events. Our attention, however, is precisely on Quantum Mechanics.

Quantum Mechanics involves the study of the behaviour of fundamental particles of an atom under different conditions and at extraordinarily high-speed using large colliders. The objective is to find the single fundamental particle that exists in all the matter. In 2012, on 4th July, at CERN, Europe's Particle Physics Laboratory, scientists came out with the exciting news of the 'Higgs Boson,' some even called it the God Particle. But it failed to provide many crucial answers including its own mass or the mass of dark matter. Even the dual behaviour as 'wave' and 'particle' remains a myth or at least unpredictable. However, it has established one thing: **all forms of matter are 'solidified light,' i.e., Energy as in $E = mc^2$ and the electromagnetic force holds all atoms together.**

So, where do we go from here? Yoga is energy itself and pervades everything, manifested, and unmanifested. It is the primal source for creation, sustenance, dissolution, and recreation of the cosmos and all that is in it in a cyclical fashion. Physics, through its celebrated theory of quantum mechanics establishes that all matter is nothing but solidified energy. What is the difference then? May be the methodology.

Both believe in the concept of energy. Science through a collective empirical observation, mathematical modelling, logical philosophy and/or experiment using external tools and equipment. And yoga through a collection of individual accounts using self as the tool. Both believe in the theory of energy as the means as well as the goal. Both desire to know the Absolute Truth.

Science possibly acknowledges the truth, but as a discipline, will find it difficult to state it so. The great similarity that I see in the yogic approach and the theory of quantum mechanics is the role of tiniest constituents that make up matter including the human body and mind. According to quantum mechanics, these small matters made of tiny particles, are bound together by a force they call, electromagnetic force. Yoga calls that force as *pran*. I shall have the least hesitation in ascribing the name quantum yoga so long as we accept that the binding force in all matters is energy.

No clearer mention of *Yoga Shakti* (yoga as Universal Energy) can be found anywhere else than the following pronouncement of **Lord Krishna, also known as Yogeshwa**r amongst His various names in *Bhagavad Gita*, Chapter 11.

*Na tu mum shakyase drasthum, anen swa chakshusha,*
*Divyam dadami te chakchuh, pashamev yogam aishwaram*

(You cannot see me with your normal vision; therefore, I grant you the Divine vision to

Enable you see my infinite form expanded **through *yoga shakti*).**

Thus, we see how science and yoga converge in acknowledging the underlying principle of energy as the cause of all that can be seen, perceived, and beyond. Science, through the most celebrated theory of quantum mechanics, and yoga through personal experience, manifestation, and revelation by the enlightened souls.

Further testimony to the convergence theory is effectively stated by the acknowledged Yoga *Guru* of the contemporary era, Sri B. K. S. Iyengar in his book, *Light on Yoga Sutras of Patanjali*, and I quote:

*Prana* is an auto-energizing force which creates a magnetic field in the form of the Universe at all levels. It acts as physical energy; as mental energy, where the mind gathers information; and as intellectual energy. This same *Prana* acts as sexual energy, spiritual energy, and cosmic energy. All that vibrates in the Universe is *Prana*: heat, light, gravity, magnetism, vigour, power, vitality, electricity, life, and spirit are all forms of *Prana*. It is the cosmic personality, potent in all beings and non-beings. It is the prime mover of activity.

This paper will be incomplete without the views expressed by Adi Shankaracharya (8th century AD). He provided the dynamism and all-encompassing nature of Hinduism. His theory of Advait became the cornerstone of Brahman belief. He asserted that Brahman is the Pure Consciousness, and that the Pure Consciousness is the Absolute Reality. It will be of interest to see Shankaracharya's views about the Universe vis-a-vis the quantum physics of today.

We shall use the abbreviation A.S. for Adi Shankaracharya and Q.P. for quantum physics.

About the universe:

A.S *'Brahman Satya, jagat Mithya'* - The Brahman is absolute reality, the universe is a destructible mirage.

Q.P. Only consciousness is real that exists. Rest is destructible.

A.S. The universe is created and dissolved, cyclical nature of manifestation and annihilation. It is borne of Brahman and disappears in Him.

Q.P. The atoms are the building block of the universe and the entire constituents that are a part of the universe, the sun, the stars, the planets, etc. In the end, all these disappear and merge into consciousness.

A.S. *Jivatma* (soul) is part of the Super (soul), the Brahman. Ignorance is the cause of strive one makes to merge with the Supreme Soul.

Q.P. Everyone was once part of one consciousness. Later, it separated. In the end, all will merge back into one.

On Liberation:

A.S. On liberation, the individual transcends time, space, and mind.

Q.P. When someone deeply understands that consciousness, then there is no time, no space, and no mind.

On Mind:

A.S. Because he can think (the function of mind), a person feels he is different and separate.

Q.P. Individuality is an illusion caused by the mind.

On Realisation of Brahman:

A.S. Brahman cannot be realised through senses owing to their limitations.

Q.P. Infinity cannot be realised through finite mediums.

A.S. and Q.P. conclude that:

The entire Universe is one consciousness. We perceive and experience differently because of our different *karmas*. Death is an illusion. Life is eternal. The Truth is one. Some call God. Some others call it energy (*Shakti*). Scientists/philosophers call it consciousness.

In conclusion, we can say:

***Quantum Yoga will be the natural binding force between oriental religious philosophy and the world of Science. These are mutually***

*compatible. The final meeting point will be when Science comes out with a modified Theory of Relativity where the Universe will be infinite and there will be a form of energy travelling at an infinite speed. Then we shall have a theory that will require no further amendment, alteration, and replacement. We shall have a theory without probability and binding conditions. The concept of 'nonlocality 'is a move in that direction .*

# REFERENCE

1. Srimad Bhagwat Gita.
2. Venkatesananda, Swami. *The Supreme Yoga, Yoga Vasistha*. Motilal Banarsidass Publishers, 2010.
3. Saraswati, Swami Yogeswaranand. *Science of Soul*. Navin, 1987.
4. Maharishi, Ramana. *Maha Yoga and Who Am I*. Sri Ramanasramam Tiruvannamalai, 2002.
5. Capra, Fritjof. *The Tao of Physics*. HarperCollins, 2007.
6. Weiss, Brian. *Many Lives, Many Masters*. Piatkus, 1994.
7. Livio, Mario. *Is God a Mathematician*. Simon & Schuster, 2010.
8. Zohar, Danah. *The Quantum Self*. William Morrow Paperbacks, 1991.
9. Iyengar, B. K. S. *Yoga: The Path to Holistic Health*. DK Illustrated, 2007.
10. Iyengar, B. K. S. *Light on Yoga*. Schocken, 1995.
11. Iyengar, B. K. S. *Light on Yoga Sutras of Patanjali*. Thorsons, 2002.

12. Iyengar, B. K. S. *Light on Pranayam.* Element, 2005.

13. Tulsidas, Goswami. *Ramcharitmanas.* (Publisher, Year of Publication)

14. Roy, B. N. *Yoga, You and God.* (Publisher, Year of Publication)

15. Roy, B. N. *Jiva, Jivatma, Parmatma evam Yoga.* (Publisher, Year of Publication)

# SOME SELECTED YOGA POSTURES

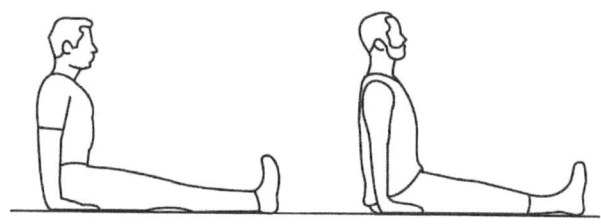

**DANDASANA**

**SUKHASANA**

**SIRASANA**

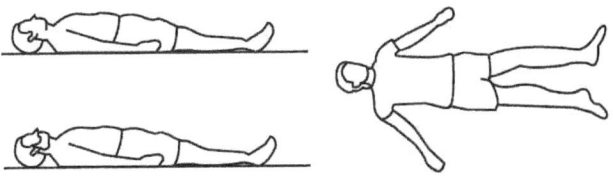

**SAVASANA**

**PADMASANA**

www.ingramcontent.com/pod-product-compliance
Ingram Content Group UK Ltd.
Pitfield, Milton Keynes, MK11 3LW, UK
UKHW022235230426